THE TRAVEL CHAMPION

A 4-Step Guide to Traveling the World Solo,

Safely, and on a Budget

Cicely F. Mitchell

Published in the United States by THE TRAVEL CHAMPION, Cartersville, GA – <www.thetravelchampion.com>

First The Travel Champion Edition, 2021

First Printing

Paperback ISBN: 978-1-7376353-0-7

eBook ISBN: 978-1-7376353-1-4

Library of Congress Cataloguing-in-Publication Data:

Mitchell, Cicely F.

The travel champion: a 4-step guide to traveling the world solo, safely, and on a budget / Cicely F. Mitchell

Library of Congress Control Number: 2021917507

The content provided in this book is for informational purposes only. The comprised information does not constitute professional travel and/or financial advice for your particular situation. The information contained in this book is no substitute for direct expert assistance, and if such assistance is required, the services of a competent professional should be sought. Websites and published work referenced in this book are provided for the reader's convenience only and does not embody official approval or endorsement of any party, product, or service, and the author makes no warranties or representation as to the accuracy or completeness of the information provided by these sources. To the maximum extent permitted by law, the publisher and author disclaim any and all liability in the event any information, commentary, analysis, opinions, advice, and/or recommendations included in this book prove to be inaccurate, incomplete, or unreliable. Though every effort has been made to supply accurate information at the time of publication, certain terms, conditions, offers, or other material information may change over time. Neither the publisher nor author is responsible for any legal, financial, medical, or other hardships caused by acting on the information provided in this book. The publisher and the author are providing this book and its contents on an "as is" basis. Please perform your own research and due diligence and utilize the information provided at your own risk.

To my parents Marshall and Shelia Mitchell,

who exposed me to travel at an early age through family road trips and vacations,

I dedicate this book.

I love you and appreciate the support you have always given me.

Table of Contents

Preface

Over the years, I have had several people familiar with my experience in travel suggest I write a book. I must admit I had kept the idea in the back of my mind as something I might do later in life once I had traveled the world extensively and was ready to settle down a bit. As of now, I have visited all fifty states in America, all seven continents, and over thirty countries, and I am currently making my way through the New 7 Wonders of the World with just two remaining. Frankly, I have no plans of settling down anytime soon. I have, however, come to the realization that it may be beneficial for me to share my travel experience with others in the form of a guidebook to help beginner and intermediate solo travelers interested in planning their own trips. I figure now is as good a time as any for me to embark upon this endeavor.

When I set out to write this book, I pondered over how to ensure the content would be relevant for the intended audience. In other words, I needed to identify the key barriers that cause people to shy away from solo travel and address those barriers.

Well, first of all, I would say the biggest obstacle people face is fear. Some are afraid to travel solo because they are concerned about their safety. They have listened to friends, family, co-workers, and/or classmates who hardly ever go anywhere warn them about the horrific dangers of traveling alone.

Others are uneasy about solo travel because they encounter loneliness traveling by themselves. They enjoy traveling but have only done so with others and feel more comfortable in a couple or group setting.

Often, people are hesitant to travel, period (solo or with others), because they believe you have to be rich or retired to travel. In their minds, they don't have enough money or time to travel.

There is yet another possible category. A huge barrier for some is the sense of not being qualified or adequately prepared to plan a successful trip. They are willing and eager to go anywhere in the world, but they don't feel like they have enough information or the information that they have is not the right information. Namely, they believe that they lack the factual data, knowledge, resources, structure, and step-by-step guidance to organize and arrange an amazing trip.

Finally, there is a population of people who desire a word of encouragement, a hint of inspiration or motivation, and evidence that it has been done before as proof that they, too, can do it. They are at the edge and are nearly ready to make the leap to solo travel; they just, perhaps, need a gentle nudge to proceed with confidence.

If you relate to any of these scenarios, then I have great news for you. This book is for you! This book tackles every one of these situations and so much more. Through knowledge, research, and personal experience, I share with you information, instructions, practical examples, recommendations, and advice to guide you through the process of successfully planning safe solo travel anywhere you want to go!

Introduction

As I began outlining the framework for the book, I thought of how I wanted to make sure to cover all of the major questions people would generally have about safe solo domestic and international travel on a budget. That includes the Why, Where, When, What, and How of it all. So, this is the premise for the layout of the book.

I start by discussing *Why*. Why travel? Why am I writing this book? This lays the foundation for the narrative and expresses the inspiration behind the book.

I then lead into the first step of the guide by addressing *Where* and *When*. When you mention you have a big trip planned, there are typically two questions people ask you first: 1) Where are you going? 2) When are you going? In this step, I provide lots of information and advice about how to determine your travel destination and the best time to go.

Next comes *How*. Once you know where and when you want to go, it makes sense to focus on how you will get there and how you will get around while you're there. So, Step Two is centered on deciding your method(s) of transportation and scheduling accordingly.

The sequence in which you perform the final two steps is actually optional based on your personal preference. As long as they both get done, it does not matter which comes first. Nonetheless, in Step Three, attention is drawn to *What*. Well, when you plan on going somewhere, it is good to have a general idea of what you are going to do while you are there. In this section, I share ideas and examples of things to do on your trip.

Last, but not least, I wrap up with another important *Where*. Where are you going to stay? In Step Four, I walk through some common lodging choices while presenting pros and cons and comparisons and contrasts.

Throughout the steps, I offer economical alternatives and hacks for saving money and being budget conscious as you plan your trip. Additionally, I provide you with several safety tips for solo traveling so that you are prepared and protected.

Alright now, let's get started!

Why Travel?

"The world is a book, and those who do not travel read only one page."

– Saint Augustine

Travel enlarges your mind, access, and perception of your existence in this world. It grants you exposure to new and diverse cultures. You have an opportunity to get a glimpse of how different people speak, think, eat, believe, work, play, and live. Exploring the world has personally broadened my horizons and expanded my views on many topics, as I now see things from a more comprehensive perspective. Whether you are taking a three-day weekend trip to a city a couple of states over or you are spending a week or two in a country on the other side of the world, you have a chance to take in new sights, scenes, scents, sounds, situations, flavors, festivals, and fiestas. It can be educational, entertaining, exhilarating, emotional, relaxing, healing, and even life-altering.

You must remember that your travel experience is what you make of it.

Being a solo globetrotter has been beneficial, as it has forced me to step outside my comfort zone on several occasions. No matter how much I plan in advance, when on vacation, there are inevitably situations I encounter or decisions I must make on the fly. It doesn't necessarily have to be anything serious. It can be something simple like trying to figure out where I'm going to eat dinner and how to get there. Or, it can be a circumstance like dealing with lost luggage. As a result, I have developed a spirit of adaptability, resourcefulness, spontaneity, and creativity. Sometimes, I have been able to figure things out by myself, and other times, I have had to reach out and rely on others for help. In either case, I have come out on the other side stronger and better.

From having a casual conversation turned networking opportunity in a restaurant in Beijing with Londoners to socializing with three lovely German women I met on a boat in the Mexico Rocks in Belize as we prepared to snorkel among the coral reefs and swim with sharks, I have had some remarkable interactions. Sometimes, when I am far away from home, I feel freer to converse with strangers. The fact that they don't know me gives me an air of liberation, for I'm not confined or defined by my day-to-day identity, vocation, or personality. Essentially, I can be whoever I want to be in that moment. It gives me a sense of courage I wouldn't normally possess. Over time, that expression of boldness has gradually seeped into my subconscious, as I have noticed with each trip, I return home less inhibited and more open and outgoing in social, professional, and personal situations, which is a treasured improvement.

Taking a trip allows you to get a break from reality. You may be fleeing from the rat race of Corporate America or the mundane day-to-day schedule of being a stay-at-home parent. In either scenario, it is good to get away every now and then in order to return refreshed, restored, and refocused.

There have been times when an excursion has served as a source of therapy for me, affording a mental break from a stressful or intense situation. The brief escape helped me maintain my sanity and reestablish balance.

Relatedly, there is a considerable amount of research that suggests that traveling the world is highly valuable for your physical, mental, and emotional health. Based on a joint study from the Global Commission on Aging and Transamerica Center for Retirement Studies, in partnership with the U.S. Travel Association, traveling truly keeps you healthier. "The study found that women who vacation at least twice a year show a significantly lower risk of suffering a heart attack than those who only travel every six years or so. The same is true for men. Men who do not take an annual vacation show a 20 percent higher risk of death and 30 percent greater risk of heart disease."[1]

In other research, travel has been identified as a potentially healthier alternative to medication for "escaping the hopelessness of a depressed state. A study from the Marshfield Clinic in Wisconsin found that women who vacation at least twice a year are less likely to suffer from depression and chronic stress than women who vacation less than once every two years."[2]

Finally, while it is likely not surprising that the majority of people tend to be happier when they are traveling without having to worry about work, it may be interesting to discover that according to a Cornell University study, "people also experience a direct increase in happiness from just planning a trip. The study found that the anticipation of taking a vacation is far greater than the anticipation of acquiring a physical possession. Thus, the benefits of traveling abroad begin well before the trip does."[3]

So, let's get to planning your next trip!

---

[1] Alton, "Health Benefits."
[2] Ibid.
[3] Ibid.

Why Am I Writing this Book?

<u>Wanderlust</u>

wanderlust (ˈwɒn dər ˌlʌst) n. A strong, innate desire to rove or travel about.

I absolutely love to travel!!! There is no other experience like it in the world. I enjoy visiting new places, seeing, learning about, and doing new things, and meeting new people. I have been blessed to have had some amazing adventures in m y relatively short lifetime thus far, and I look forward to many more as long as I am alive and kicking.

I believe my love for travel began when I was a youth and my family went on trips for Spring Break and during the summer for vacation. My parents took turns driving as my brother and I sat in the back seat of the family car during road trips from Arkansas to places like New Orleans, Louisiana; St. Louis, Missouri; Denver, Colorado; San Antonio, Texas; and Washington, D.C.

Though I rode in eager anticipation of arriving at our travel destination, I also relished the journey along the way. Countless times, my little brother would be asleep within fifteen minutes of beginning our trip. My dad gave him the nickname "City

Limits," as my brother would be knocked out by the time we left our hometown and crossed over to the next city. I, on the other hand, did not like taking naps because I didn't want to miss a thing! There are times I recall fighting drooping eyelids because I was trying to stay awake to take in everything. From a young age, I was very curious about the world around me, and I looked forward to exploring as much of it as I could.

During the summer after my junior year of high school, I had my first opportunity to travel abroad. I was fortunate to participate in a foreign exchange program that my high school French teacher had coordinated for a few students at my school and another school in the region. Earlier, in the spring of that year, a young lady from France lived with my family and me for about a couple weeks, and now it was time for me to travel to France to live with her family during the summer. Not only was it my first time leaving the country, but it was also my first time on an airplane! Because of this, I was a little nervous and insecure, excited, and humbled.

We flew from Little Rock Municipal Airport to Cincinnati/Northern Kentucky International Airport and then to Europe. From the moment we arrived at Paris Charles de Gaulle Airport, I could sense an immediate shift in the environment. Of course, the most obvious change was the language, as we could hear French spoken all around us. Amidst the hustle and bustle of people rushing from here to there in the airport, not only did I notice the difference in sights and scents, but there was also a transition in the overall feel or "vibe" of the place. It was not necessarily better or worse than my typical environment; it was just different. I found all these differences to be quite intriguing.

As I spent time at my new temporary home with my host family, attended classes at the local high school with my exchange student, and hung out at cafés, the cinema, and discothèque with my exchange student and her friends and my friends from my high school back home who were also part of the exchange, I got a chance to be immersed in the French culture. This occasion was both interesting and eye-opening. While in France, I also got an opportunity to visit many famous landmarks like the Eiffel Tower, the Louvre, the Notre-Dame Cathedral, and the Arc de Triomphe. My fellow exchange students and I walked along the Champs-Élysées singing "Les Champs-Élysées." What a fun and memorable time! Seeing places firsthand that I had previously only read about in books or seen on television was an awesome experience! A spirit of wanderlust had been ignited and would forever remain aflame.

Travel Goals

"I haven't been everywhere, but it's on my list."
– Susan Sontag

Upon graduating from college in Tennessee, I accepted a job about thirty miles north of Boston, Massachusetts and about fifteen minutes from the New Hampshire border. Prior to flying in to interview for this job, I had never been to New England. Since there were several states in the area I hadn't visited within driving distance, I devised a goal to explore all the New England states while I was living up that way. Then, I decided I would go to the Mid-Atlantic states. Not too long after accomplishing those travel goals, I began to contemplate, *Why not visit all fifty states?* Thus, this became my goal.

After having enjoyed several trips around the country and I had about seventeen or so states remaining that I had not visited, I was having a conversation with a friend of mine from college. He used to call me "World Traveler" because at this time, in addition to having visited approximately 65 percent of the states in America, I had also visited about ten countries. My friend jokingly asked, "So, Miss World Traveler, after you visit all fifty states, what are you going to do? Visit all seven continents?!" We both laughed and laughed for about a solid minute. Then, I began to think, *Hmm, that's actually not a bad idea.* Hence, that became my next big travel goal.

At the time of writing this book, I have visited all fifty states, all seven continents, and about thirty countries, so I have an accumulated wealth of applied knowledge. Over two-thirds of my international trips, I conquered solo, and I planned nearly 90 percent of those trips myself. Regardless of my income at the time of each trip, I managed to stay within budget and had some truly amazing and memorable experiences. Throughout my decades of travel, I have learned tremendous amounts of information, hacks, and tips that I am enthusiastic about sharing with other eager travelers in the form of this planning guide.

Excuses, Excuses

"The man who goes alone can start today; but he who travels with another must wait till that other is ready."

– Henry David Thoreau

As I was traveling the country and the world, many times I would travel with family, friends, classmates, or colleagues. I enjoyed traveling with others but often ended up traveling alone because no one was available, willing, or able to travel when I wanted to go to a particular place. People would often rattle off excuses about not being able to afford to travel, not having the time to travel, not wanting to go somewhere different that may be outside of their comfort zone, not having someone to watch their kids or pets, or any other number of things. The only reason I refer to them as excuses is because whenever I would propose solutions for the issues they presented, they would only offer additional reasons or "excuses" for why they couldn't go. I came to the realization that people are generally going to make a way to do whatever it is that they really want to do.

Travel is a priority for me, so I have learned how to do what I need to do in order to make it happen. I cannot allow my travel experience to be diminished or nonexistent because I am waiting around on people to travel with who are always going to have some excuse as to why they can't travel because travel is not a priority for them. I cannot permit myself to be discouraged about the amount of time I have available to travel because my job only gives me a limited amount of vacation days or PTO (paid time off) per year. Though I am not a millionaire with huge sums of money to blow, I refuse to be bound in town when I desire to be somewhere across the world. I am sure that many of you can relate. All these circumstances can be addressed with the proper planning, preparation, and mindset, and this book will help walk you through it.

"Solo," "World," "Budget," and "Champion" Defined

Though the title of this book may seem to be pretty self-explanatory, I feel the need to define a few key terms. When many hear the word "solo," they tend to think of the word "alone." While they are, in fact, synonyms, you can be traveling solo in a group. For instance, you can plan a trip where you are traveling to a destination by yourself, but once you arrive, you join a group of people you have never before met. Technically, you are still solo even though you are among others. This book pertains to people in both solo categories. Whether you are truly traveling alone, mountain hiking in Alaska or you are by yourself in Bali in the midst of others at a yoga retreat, this book is for you. Actually, the information shared in this book can be applied by couples, families, large groups, or anyone else seeking to travel who finds the information relevant. However, I will be providing some tips that are especially critical for solo travelers, particularly as it relates to safety.

Traveling the world can mean that you are taking a month-long trip to a faraway continent or a day trip to a city a few miles from you. The guidelines and advice shared in this book can be implemented for both domestic and international travel. You can even employ some of the information to plan a nice staycation. It is whatever your pleasure.

Dictonary.com defines a budget as "the total sum of money set aside or needed for a purpose." With that stated, the specific amount of money set aside can vary vastly depending on one's income or financial situation. While the budget of a billionaire CEO likely differs significantly from that of a blue-collar employee working a nine-to-five job, it is a budget, nonetheless. This book will reveal ways to plan economically and have an enjoyable travel experience, regardless of your income bracket.

The word "champion" has a dual meaning. Of course, it can be a winner, hero/heroine, or warrior, but it can also be an advocate, defender, or strong supporter. As a travel champion, I am a huge proponent of people getting out and exploring the planet in which we live because, as previously expressed, I recognize the enormous benefits one can gain from doing so.

I also realize that there is nothing more exhilarating and satisfying than conquering the world and enjoying the journey.

By reading and employing the strategies outlined in this book, I know you, too, will fully embody the essence of a travel champion.

STEP ONE – Determine Where and When to Go

"Wherever you go becomes a part of you somehow."

– Anita Desai

N ow that you know why you should travel and that there is nothing that can really prevent you from traveling, let's talk about how to determine where and when to travel. I group *where* and *when* together because they are somewhat linked with one another as part of the planning process.

Eight Factors for Selecting a Travel Destination

There are several important factors that must be considered when selecting a travel destination. I will be highlighting eight factors that should be examined individually and collectively based on your personal experience and comfort level. Some of these are listed because they are things you should simply be aware of as you begin putting together your wish list of travel destinations. They will not necessarily make or break your decision to visit a certain place but will allow you to be more informed as you make your decision and plan your itinerary. Other factors will aid you in gauging how comfortable or safe you may feel in a particular environment. Last but not least, a good portion of these factors are included to help you home in on exactly when you should travel to your destination of choice and give you a glimpse into the planning and preparation that will need to take place in advance. The list is in no specific sequence. With that said, the first factor being contemplated is culture.

1. Culture

Per lifescience.com, culture is "the characteristics and knowledge of a particular group of people."[4] The Center for Advanced Research on Language Acquisition defines culture as "shared patterns of behaviors and interactions, cognitive constructs and understanding that are learned by socialization...the growth of a group identity fostered by social

---

[4] Zimmermann, "What Is Culture?"

patterns unique to the group."[5] Cristina De Rossi, an anthropologist at Barnet and Southgate College in London states that "culture encompasses religion, food, what we wear, how we wear it, our language, marriage, music, what we believe is right or wrong, how we sit at the table, how we greet visitors, how we behave with loved ones, and a million other things."[6] For this book, as it relates to travel destination selection, we will focus on reviewing four aspects of culture: language, cuisine, religion and politics, and ethnicity and social beliefs.

Language

Depending on your knowledge and education, experience, adaptability, and/or comfortability, language difference may or may not be a big deal to you. Either way, you should at least be aware of the official language(s) spoken in your prospective travel destination.

Some people only choose to visit places where their native language is the predominate language spoken, and this is acceptable. It's a personal decision. I would, however, like to encourage you to gradually step outside of your comfort zone in order to expand your options if language is your only deterrent for visiting a particular location. For example, if English is your

---

[5] Ibid.
[6] Ibid.

native language and you are from the United States, obviously, you can visit the United Kingdom, but you can also branch out to visit places where English is not the official language but frequently spoken and understood due to high levels of tourism. When I was in Tokyo, Japan, just about everybody spoke and understood English even though the official language is Japanese. I was able to experience a very different culture in Tokyo compared to that of the United States but was able to make my way through the city with relative ease speaking only English.

It is helpful to know some common words and phrases in the official language of the country you are visiting, such as *yes*, *no*, *hello*, *thank you*, *bathroom*, *where*, and *how much*. There are numerous apps where you can learn a basic conversational level of a foreign language in preparation for your trip. A few popular free apps include Duolingo, MemRise, Babbel, Busuu, and HelloTalk.

Also, there are language apps that you can download for reference purposes to translate printed text. Google Translate offers a feature where you can actually scan or take a picture of some words or phrases, and it will translate it for you into your desired language available in the app. This is helpful for translating signs and menus. I have personally benefited from this feature on multiple occasions. Another helpful translation app is Linguee. It is free and can be utilized offline, so you do not have to rely on having Wi-Fi in order to access it.

Cuisine

Now, everybody knows that food is important, right? You've got to eat in order to live. Personally, I think it is great to venture out and try different dishes as you travel, especially local cuisine that is exclusive to a particular region. I recognize that some people are timid when it comes to their taste buds, and I can relate at times. Some food may not look or smell like what we are used to in our native land but may be worth trying. Who knows? You may end up falling in love with something new and different.

For those who have food allergies, during your trip planning process, a good practice is to research dishes that are popular in the area you are considering visiting to learn about their ingredients ahead of time. This way, you will know certain dishes that you will definitely need to avoid once you do visit. Of course, you will want to double-check with the server or chef at the restaurant as you are placing your order as well. Additionally, in the event that you do have an allergic reaction to something you eat, it is good to be prepared by having the proper prescriptions and medications. Make sure that you pack any medicine that you may possibly need, as sometimes it may be difficult to access these items abroad or to even effectively communicate exactly what it is that you need if there is a language barrier.

For anyone who plans on trying new cuisine at their travel destination, enjoy yourself but also have medicine available to take just in case something you eat or drink does not agree with your body. While locals who have been eating the food all of their life may be unbothered, your body may react differently to some of the diverse spices and ingredients in the food. In addition, in some parts of the world, it may not be safe for you to drink the tap water. In these cases, you should plan to have alternatives readily available, such as bottled water, and refrain from consuming ice served in drinks in restaurants as it likely consists of tap water. I reiterate that these are things that are easy to research and be prepared for in advance.

Religion and Politics

Religion and politics are two topics that people often recommend that people not discuss in public because some individuals can be very passionate, emotional, and a bit touchy when they have strong beliefs about something and those beliefs differ from others. My intent in bringing them up here is to simply suggest that you gain some general knowledge about the primary religion(s) practiced and current political climate in the area you plan to visit. This is for awareness as well as for personal safety and security.

Some places you visit internationally may require you to abide by certain religious customs when approaching a temple or sacred place. For example, before entering the main building of the Taj Mahal in India, I had to take off my shoes in an effort to prevent damage. Because I had purchased a foreign ticket to the site, I was given a pair of complimentary booties to wear. When I visited some of the sanctuaries in Bali, I was handed a cloth by staff to place over my shoulders, covering my short-sleeved top. Such customs are to be acknowledged and respected. Conversely, there are some nations where it is a crime to participate in religious activities. Gaining some basic familiarity with laws and conditions in your target travel destination will better prepare you for the environment in which you will be.

With regard to politics, a friend of mine wanted me to travel with her to a nation that we later found out was experiencing some political unrest. I believe that the travel agency she was coordinating the trip with actually ended up canceling the trip, and that is how we learned of the chaotic scene. On another occasion, I was in a foreign city where the citizens were protesting in the streets because they were displeased with their government officials. The protesting was relatively peaceful, so I did not feel threatened or like I was in danger. Though, I must admit that it helped that a few of the locals had made me aware of the protests the day before, so I was not caught off guard.

I share these stories not to make you afraid but to make you aware, so you are able to prepare as much as you can. As you organize, I recommend that you seek information from reliable sources like the U.S. Department of State Travel Advisory prior to your trip and reputable news outlets while at your destination. Family, friends, co-workers, and classmates who do not travel are typically NOT who you should seek for advice and counsel about these matters because you will almost always be bombarded with negativity and discouragement. I know this from personal experience and through feedback from countless fellow solo travelers. People who have not traveled much and/or are scared to travel are merely sharing their opinions with you; it is not based on facts, evidence, or experience. They usually don't mean any harm, but they are often speaking from a place of fear and will project that fear onto you if you allow them to do so.

Be cautious, but be cautious based on facts and research, not opinions and unwarranted horror.

Ethnicity, Physical Appearance, and Social Beliefs

Similar to the previous two topics, ethnicity, physical appearance, and social beliefs are subjects people tend to shy away from discussing much publicly; nevertheless, I would be remiss if I didn't touch upon these topics here. Categories such as ethnicity, nationality, race, color, gender, age, sexual identity, sexual orientation, marital status, and disability are often associated with different views and sentiments depending on where you are in the world. For example, there are certain regions of the world where Americans are not viewed favorably. In a number of cultures, women are treated as inferior. There are some places where there is hatred and disdain for people of the LGBTQ (Lesbian, Gay, Bisexual, Transgender, Queer) community. For these reasons, it is good to be aware of how these categories or related categories are viewed in destinations you are considering visiting. In selected cases, for you specifically, it may mean that it is not safe to visit the location during a particular time or maybe at any time in the foreseeable future. In other instances, it may be okay to visit, but you should be cautious and vigilant in certain parts of town. You must always be aware and alert in general as a solo traveler. Once more, I do not want you to be fearful, but I do want you to be informed and prepared.

As I strolled through the streets of Shanghai, China, I caught a few natives sneakily snapping random photos of me. Being that I was a young African-American woman with braids, I stood out. Apparently, they were intrigued by my appearance and wanted to capture the moment.

Not everyone was as discreet. At one point, I was standing in front of a building, gazing into a crowd, when out of nowhere, this Asian lady walked up to me, stood her toddler son beside me, and backed up to take a picture. I immediately tried to move out of the frame because I didn't want to photo bomb the picture the lady was trying to take of her son. I thought she stood him beside me to let me know that she was trying to take a picture and she wanted me to move out of the way.

When I attempted to clear the space, she began motioning to me to get back in the frame and telling her son to smile. It was only then that I realized that she wanted me to be in the picture. Since neither of them spoke directly to me and I had never seen them before, it was a bit of a peculiar situation to me. Honestly, I found it a little funny because it was so odd. I was a good sport about it. After I smiled and posed for a few snapshots with her son, the lady bowed her head in gratitude and grabbed her son's hand as they scurried away and disappeared back into the crowd. I was literally left standing there shaking my head and chuckling to myself as I thought, *What just happened?*

I have heard fellow African-American women swap similar stories of their experiences in China. Some thoroughly enjoyed the attention, feeling like celebrities being lauded by eager photographers at a red-carpet premier event. Others described an altogether different scene where they felt harassed and as though their privacy was being invaded. Because of this, they were uncomfortable and hesitant to be out and about in town by themselves. In circumstances like these, it is challenging to predict exactly how you may react. However, if you know in advance a little about the environment and culture of a place, you can utilize that information as you decide whether or not to visit a particular location or how you should mentally prepare yourself for the blatant stares, devoted interest, and/or awkward interactions. You should never intentionally put yourself in harm's way or in a setting where you may experience anxiety or the threat of physical, emotional, or social danger.

When you research your destination, take into consideration your personal perspective of safety and comfort.

Recommended Resources

There are three main sources that I suggest you utilize for gathering official country information, especially as it pertains to cultural content. These sources can be accessed through websites for the following:

- BBC Country Profiles

- The World Factbook

- U.S. Department of State Travel Country Information and Traveler Information

The British Broadcasting Corporation (BBC) publishes high-level country profiles with information about language, religion, history, and government/politics.

Providing more detailed information per country, the Central Intelligence Agency (CIA) produces The World Factbook that has data about the nation's government, geography, economy, transnational issues, and society demographics by ethnicity, language, and religion. They also supply a publication with a condensed version of this information in the form of the One-Page Summary. The World Factbook Travel Facts document is another extremely valuable resource packed with an array of data including major languages, religions, cultural practices, and whether or not there is potable water.

Last but certainly not least, there is the U.S. Department of State Travel, which serves as the primary authority for Americans traveling abroad. The site has the Country

Information section under International Travel that displays Travel Advisory levels, alerts, and information as well as any Embassy Messages. There is also a Traveler Information section within the Before You Go section under International Travel that provides guidance and resources for travelers with special considerations like Travelers with Dual Nationality, Faith-Based Travelers, U.S. Students Abroad, LGBTI Travelers, Women Travelers, Travelers with Disabilities, and Older Travelers.

In addition to reviewing those three sites as part of your research concerning the various aspects of culture, I highly recommend that you seek out Facebook groups to join and Instagram pages to follow that are specific to your needs and/or concerns. There are a plethora of groups encompassing many cross-sections. For example, you can search for groups for Jewish women travelers, Black vegan travelers, LGBTQ solo travelers, etc. The more detailed you are with the categories, the more likely the information in the group is as relevant as it can be to you. What I like about the groups is that people share firsthand experiences, so it is not like you are asking random friends and family members who do not travel for their opinions. The information and advice that people share in the groups are usually genuine and quite helpful.

2. Travel Documents

A travel document is a form of identification that a government or international treaty organization issues to citizens or visitors in order to facilitate their movement across international borders. The kind of travel document required is primarily based on what country you are from, your status in that country, what country you are traveling to, your method of entry into that country, your purpose for going there, and the amount of time you plan on staying there.

In this book, I am focusing on the most customary travel documents required by American citizens to travel to other countries. If you live in America but are not a U.S. citizen, there are other documents that may be required for you to travel abroad that I do not cover in this book. Likewise, if you are not an American citizen and you reside in a country other than the United States, you will need to take the time to examine what travel documents are needed in order for you to travel to foreign countries from your home country, as they are not highlighted in this book.

So, let's start out by discussing the most widely known type of travel document for Americans to travel internationally – the passport.

Passports

Locations Where a Passport Is Not Needed

As an American, you do not need a U.S. passport to travel to any of the fifty states or any of the U.S. territories like Puerto Rico, Guam, American Samoa, the U.S. Virgin Islands, and the Northern Mariana Islands. You should, however, plan to travel with your valid government issued identification such as a driver's license or U.S. military ID.

If you are seeking to travel to locations in the Caribbean other than the aforementioned as part of a cruise that starts and ends in the United States, all you are required to have is a birth certificate and a valid government-issued ID. When you participate in these closed-loop cruises, the ship docks in cities that do not require you to present a passport. Some of these destinations include cities in the Bahamas, Bermuda, Costa Rica, Jamaica, Mexico, Belize, and Honduras. This is great because there are several international places where you can take a spur-of-the-moment trip to enjoy your fun in the sun without a passport.

Applying for a Passport

If you are a U.S. citizen and you are planning to travel internationally by air, land, or sea and you are not part of a closed-loop cruise, you will at the very least need a passport card or passport book. A passport card is used for entering the United States at land-border crossings and seaports-of-entry from Canada, Mexico, the Caribbean, or Bermuda. The passport card **cannot be used for international air travel**. A passport book (commonly referred to as simply a "passport") is used for international travel by air, sea, or land.[7]

For individuals sixteen years old or older, passport cards and books are valid for ten years. For those under age sixteen, passport cards and books are valid for five years. For first-time applicants sixteen and older, the current cost is $65 for a passport card and $145 for a passport book. For applicants under age sixteen, the current cost for a passport card is $50 and $115 for a passport book.[8] In my opinion, if you plan on taking any international flights within the next few years, it is better to go ahead and purchase the passport book versus the passport card, as you will save money in the long run.

You can apply in person at a passport acceptance facility such as a post office, clerk of court, library, or at the passport agency. According to the U.S. Department of State – Bureau of Consular Affairs, you must apply for a passport in person using Form DS-11 if <u>at least one</u> of the following statements is true:

---

[7] U.S. Department of State, "Passport Card."
[8] Ibid.

- You are applying for your first U.S. passport.

- You are under age sixteen.

- Your previous U.S. passport was issued when you were under age sixteen.

- Your previous U.S. passport was lost, stolen, or damaged.

- Your previous U.S. passport was issued more than fifteen years ago.

Please note that if you live in a country other than the U.S. (including Canada) and you are submitting Form DS-11, you are required to apply in person at a U.S. embassy or consulate.[9]

Renewing a Passport

If none of the previous statements apply to you, you may be eligible to renew your passport using Form DS-82. Even if your passport will not have expired by the time you plan to take your trip, you may need to renew it anyway. Keep in mind that most nations require that your U.S. passport has a minimum of six months of validity beyond the dates of your trip, even if you may not be intending on staying that long. Some airlines will not even allow you to board an international flight if this prerequisite is not met. You should also plan to have one or

---

[9] U.S. Department of State, "Apply in Person."

more blank pages in your passport for entry/exit stamps that will be needed. Verify the number of blank pages needed based on the requirements set forth by the country you will be visiting. This information can be found per country in the World Factbook's One-Page Summary and on the U.S. Department of State – Bureau of Consular Affairs' website.

Although you cannot utilize an expired passport for international travel, you are eligible to renew your ten-year passport within five years past the expiration date. Once the ten-year passport has been expired for five years, you are no longer able to renew it. You would have to apply in person using Form DS-11 if you wanted to obtain a new passport.[10]

If you do need to renew your passport, you may be able to do so by mail. The cost to renew a passport by mail is currently $110. Per the U.S. Department of State Travel's website, you can renew via mail if <u>ALL five</u> of the following statements are true:

- You have your passport in your possession to submit with your application.

- Your passport is not damaged other than normal wear and tear.

---

[10] U.S. Department of State, "Renew my Passport."

- Your passport was issued when you were age sixteen or older.

- Your passport was issued within the last fifteen years.

- Your passport was issued in your current name, or you can document your name change with an original or certified copy of your marriage certificate, divorce decree, or court order.

If any one of these statements is not true for you, then you must apply in person. If you reside in Canada, you may be eligible to have your passport renewed by mail and avoid a trip to the U.S. embassy or consulate. If you reside in any other nation, you are required to renew your passport at a U.S. embassy or consulate.[11]

For more information about applying for or renewing a U.S. passport card or passport book, refer to the website of the U.S. Department of State – Bureau of Consular Affairs at www.travel.state.gov.

Visas and Other Travel Documents

Aside from the passport, the visa is the next most frequently required travel document. A visa is an official document supplied by the country you wish to visit, granting you

---

[11] Ibid.

temporary permission to enter the country for a certain period of time. Some countries require you to have a visa along with your passport in order for you to enter the country. This is because the country does not have a visa policy or agreement with your home country, allowing you to travel freely between the two countries without the necessity for a visa. Other travel documents that may be required by countries or serve as alternatives to tourist visas include licenses, electronic travel authorities/authorizations, and eVisas.

Many nations' visa requirements are dependent upon the nature of your visit and the intended length of your stay. For instance, for travel to Chile, if the nature of your visit is tourism, you do not need a visa if your stay will be for ninety days or less. If you are traveling to China as a tourist, a visa is required regardless of the length of your stay. On the other hand, tourist travel to Cuba from the United States currently remains prohibited. In order to visit Cuba as an American citizen, you must obtain a license from the Department of Treasury or your purpose for travel must fit into one of twelve other categories of authorized travel such as educational activities, religious activities, humanitarian projects, or support for the Cuban people.

Time Associated with Acquiring Travel Documents

Prior to the Coronavirus and COVID-19, routine passport processing was estimated to take about six to eight weeks. If you needed your passport processed faster, you could opt for an expedited service for $60 to have it processed in two to three weeks. If you were to make an appointment and go through one of the twenty-six passport agencies or centers, you could potentially have your passport processed as quickly as eight business days.

Per their website, "to prevent the spread of COVID-19 and to protect [their] workforce and customers, the [U.S. Department of State – Bureau of Consular Affairs] significantly reduced passport operations in March 2020" (U.S. Department of State, 2020). Since then, processing times have been impacted considerably. For the most up-to-date status pertaining to estimated passport processing times, visit www.travel.state.gov.

When planning your trip, take into account travel processing times. If you are looking to plan a trip to occur within the next one to two weeks and you don't already own a passport or the one you have is expired or near expiration, you should be planning a domestic trip or a trip to somewhere that does not require a passport.

A visa is usually a label that is affixed to a page in your passport, so in order to receive the visa, you must send in your passport to have the visa attached. Because of this, when you discover that a nation you want to visit requires a visa, you must make sure you allow for enough time to send off and receive your passport back in plenty of time before your trip.

If you are an American citizen who plans to travel to Australia, you are required to have either a visa or an electronic travel authority (ETA). If you are intending to travel for tourism or business and your stay will not exceed ninety days, you are likely eligible for an ETA. An ETA provides authorization to travel to and enter Australia and is label-free and electronically linked to your passport. The customs authorities and airline check-in staff have access to your ETA using your passport details. There are a couple of benefits to going with the ETA versus the visa. First of all, the ETA for travel to Australia is cheaper than the visa, as the ETA can be purchased for under $15 USD (United States Dollars). Second, because the ETA is electronically linked to your passport, you do not have to physically mail it in to have anything attached like the visa, so this saves you time. India is another country that offers the ETA (electronic travel authorization, in this case) option for American travelers. Generally speaking, when the ETA is presented as a choice alongside the standard visa, the ETA is the better option.

Now, there are other countries that actually supply you with a visa or give you the opportunity to apply for and purchase a visa upon entering the country. This "visa on arrival" option is more convenient on the front end than the standard visa or ETA process because it requires no planning or preparation ahead of time. Nevertheless, keep in mind that there are occasional delays in acquiring the visa on arrival at some airports, so be prepared to stand in line(s). If you would prefer to minimize the delay on the back end at the destination airport, you may want to apply for a visa or eVisa during your trip planning phase if proposed as a substitute for the visa on arrival. The eVisa is an electronic visa akin to an ETA. Ethiopia, Laos, and Nepal are examples of nations that present the visa on arrival option but also give you the option to purchase a visa or eVisa in advance of your trip.

Just as there is some international travel that does not require a passport, there are some countries that do not require visas or other travel doocuments besides a passport for entry or upon arrival. Plenty of countries in Europe and South America fit into this category. As of December 2020, American citizens had visa-free access to 185 nations across the world.[12]

For more information about what travel documents are necessary for your anticipated travel destination, check out the

---

[12] Rhodes, "Travel Without a Visa."

website of the U.S. Department of State – Bureau of Consular Affairs at www.travel.state.gov.

3. Vaccinations/Immunizations

A vaccine is administered to confer immunity against a particular disease. Nations may require or recommend that visitors be vaccinated for certain diseases prior to entry within their borders. Often, these decisions are made based on where you are traveling from, where you are traveling to, and where you have recently traveled. For example, India requires a yellow fever vaccination if the traveler is arriving from an infected area. For all other travelers to India, the vaccination is suggested.[13] It is key to pay attention to the verbiage used. If it is *required*, this means that it is mandatory, and you will have to provide proof of the vaccination such as a current and valid International Certificate of Vaccination for entry. If it is *suggested* or *recommended*, it is optional, and the traveler can decide whether or not he/she wants to be vaccinated. It is a personal decision and depends on your comfort level.

For Americans seeking to travel to Madagascar, a yellow fever vaccination is required if the traveler has been in a yellow fever endemic country within six months of arrival to

---

[13] U.S. Department of State, "India International Travel Information."

Madagascar.[14] So, the restriction is not merely based on one's immediate location of departure but also the travel history over a six-month period. This is important to note, especially for frequent international travelers who may not permanently reside in a country where the vaccination is required but may have traveled to such a country within the previous six months.

I have one last example referencing the yellow fever vaccination. The U.S. Department of State indicates that the "yellow fever vaccine, documented on the WHO International Certificate of Vaccination, is required for travelers coming from Brazil, Angola, Democratic Republic of Congo, and Uganda. The vaccine must have been administered at least 10 days before arrival in Colombia."[15] While this constraint does not apply to American citizens, I am presenting this example to point out the timing associated with the vaccination requirement. If you were a citizen of any of the listed countries, you would not be able to just travel to Colombia on a whim, as you would have needed to have been vaccinated at least ten days prior to arriving in Colombia.

The previous examples mainly involve vaccination requirements based on where the individuals were traveling from and where they had recently traveled. This final example is

---

[14] U.S. Department of State, "Madagascar International Travel Information."
[15] U.S. Department of State, "Colombia International Travel Information."

focusing on the travel destination. In 2016, I planned a trip to South Africa. There was no vaccination requirement for American citizens to enter the country. However, as I was planning the trip, I learned through multiple reputable sources that there was a particular national park within South Africa that I was pondering visiting for a safari that was deemed a high-risk area for malaria during the time I was planning to visit. No vaccine exists for malaria, but there are recommended preventive measures and prescription medications. These measures and medications were not mandatory but were highly recommended, so I took them seriously. As you plan your trip, bear in mind that there may be vaccinations or prescription medications that may not be necessary for entry into a particular country but may be required or recommended for specific environments you may be visiting while in the country.

For basic information about required/recommended vaccinations, check out the Travel Facts by country within the World Factbook provided by the CIA or the Quick Facts section of Country Information within the International Travel section of the U.S. Department of State Travel website. For more detailed information regarding required/suggested vaccinations and medications broken down by region and environment, go to the website of the Centers for Disease Control (CDC) and

Prevention and search by destination under the Traveler's Health section.

4. How Much Time You Have Available for the Trip

The amount of time you have available for your trip may dictate how far you go and for how long you stay. If you only have a three-day weekend available, it makes no sense to flirt with the idea of going on a vacation from the United States to Australia because over half of your time will be spent in transit getting there and back. Unless you are going on a short cruise where the destination is not far from your location of origination and everything is already pre-planned concerning your itinerary, you are likely looking to plan a domestic trip if you only have three or fewer days available. There are certainly exceptions to this guideline. Say, for instance, you are flying in briefly to attend a special event such as a wedding or a meeting for a few hours and then returning home within a day or less. Or, maybe, you are the adventurous type, who doesn't mind being whisked away for a quick getaway for a momentary change in scenery. I can undoubtedly understand that. Nonetheless, most people under normal circumstances would not plan to travel abroad to a far destination for a weekend trip. If you have four days or more, it is doable to leave the country for a trip. Just make sure that you plan your mode of transportation carefully. We will discuss this more in the next step.

If you have a week or more available, it is within reason to plan a trip to visit multiple places whether that is multiple states in the United States, multiple cities within the same foreign country, or even multiple countries that are within relatively close proximity of one another. If you are traveling to the Caribbean, Europe, or Asia, logistically, it is very easy to visit multiple countries within the same trip. It may just be a matter of taking a ferry or the metro or possibly renting a car.

During your planning phase, as you research the travel documents needed for your main travel destination, don't forget to also check out necessary documents for entry to your excursion or side trip destinations.

If you are planning on visiting multiple destinations (i.e., cities, states, countries, or continents), put some thought into how much time you would like to stay in each location. Part of this is dependent upon your travel goals and objectives. If you are seeking to check as many places as you can off your bucket list, you may want to cram in a bunch of locations to cover as much territory as sanely possible. If this is your plan, I recommend that you take plenty of pictures (and maybe a few notes) because when you visit a myriad of similar places back-to-back, they all tend to run together after a while. If when you return, people ask you a lot of questions about each specific place you went, you want to be able to distinguish in your mind one place from another for them and for yourself.

Also, on a side note, if you plan on following the travel bucket list cramming strategy, especially if there is a substantial time difference between your last travel destination on your trip and your home location, you may want to take it a little easy on the last day of your trip or allow a day or more when you return to recover, as jet lag is a very real phenomenon for some people. Sometimes, people are so exhausted when they return from a trip that they feel like they need a vacation after their vacation! If this is you or you aren't sure if it is you or not because you have not traveled much internationally, plan to factor in some time for recuperation. On the other hand, if you know for a fact that this is not you, I say YOLO (you only live once); have at it!!

If you do not have a travel goal to check off as many places as you can on a bucket list, perhaps, you may want to spend more time in a particular location versus ripping and running to multiple locations. There is no right or wrong travel goal. It is a personal thing based on what is important to you. I know people who like to spend a month in one location. This gives them the opportunity to fully immerse themselves in the culture of the place. When you spend more time in a location, you move past taking pictures at popular tourist sites to stepping off the beaten path and living among the locals. You have a chance to explore, meet new people, and try different things. These types of experiences can lead to lifelong memories and friendships. So, if you are curious and/or adventurous, whether you are an outgoing person or an introvert willing to step outside of your comfort zone and you have adequate time available, it may be worth your while to spend a decent amount of time somewhere. I'm sure you will be glad that you did.

For those of you who are currently employed and have a limited amount of vacation time or PTO, I would like to propose a few hacks to help you make the most of your time off. Early in my career, I only had two weeks (10 eight-hour days) of vacation time and no sick days. So, I learned how to be creative in managing and scheduling my vacation time, and even though I now have more time available, I still use some of the same hacks to maximize the time I have available for trips.

Tip number one is to schedule your vacation time around weekends and holidays, especially if the holiday falls on a Monday or Friday. This allows you to stretch your overall time off. For instance, at my current job, we get Thanksgiving Thursday and the Friday after off as paid holidays. So, I have that Thursday, Friday, Saturday, and Sunday off. I could take the Monday, Tuesday, and Wednesday off leading up to Thanksgiving. If I were to leave town on the Saturday morning before Thanksgiving, I would have that Saturday through

Sunday of the next week available for a trip. That is nine days off with only using up three vacation days! Do you know how many places I could visit in nine days?! SEVERAL!! Depending on the location, I could spend a few days in three different cities in the same state, multiple cities in three different states, or two to three different countries on the same continent or on two different continents.

A few years ago, I took a trip to Asia in November. Though I had nineteen days available for my trip, I only had to take eleven days off for vacation. I left home the Wednesday morning the week before Thanksgiving and returned the Saturday afternoon the week after Thanksgiving. During that timeframe, I visited four countries – China, Thailand, Myanmar, and India. Within those four nations, I visited ten cities. I decided to give myself a day and a half to recuperate by having the Saturday afternoon and all day Sunday at home before returning to work Monday morning. This was mainly because I had done a lot of ripping and running while I was traveling in Asia and during that time, I operated in three different time zones – one that was twelve hours ahead of my home time zone, one that was eleven hours ahead of my home time zone, and one that was nine-and-a-half hours ahead of my home time zone. Yes, half-hour increment differences exist in India. When it is 4:30 PM on Monday in New York, it is 2 AM on Tuesday in New Delhi. So, anyway, I wanted to make sure to allow some time for me to rest and to account for potential jet lag that I might experience.

Tip number two for extending your available travel time when you have limited PTO or vacation time is to take an evening flight or drive to your destination right after work. If you have a three-day weekend where you are off work for a Friday holiday plus the Saturday and Sunday, you could book a 6:45 PM flight out on Thursday after work as opposed to taking a Friday morning flight. This way, depending on your destination, you could arrive by late Thursday night and already be there to enjoy a full day on Friday.

Tip number three would be to utilize half days off or quarter days off work if your company allows you to do so. For instance, if you work from 9 AM to 5 PM, it may be a stretch for you to leave work at 5 PM to catch a 6:45 PM flight if you take into advisement travel time in rush hour traffic, not to mention accounting for time to park (if you drive to the airport) and make your way through security at the airport. In this scenario, you may ponder taking a quarter day off of PTO, (i.e., two hours off), to allow yourself a couple more hours so you are not cutting things too close. This way, you still have 75 percent of a PTO day left that you can use at a later time.

Partial vacation days can also be used to give yourself a little extra time off when you return from a trip. Say, for example, you have a flight returning home late Sunday night and you know that it will be a struggle for you to get up to go in early Monday morning; you can schedule to have that Monday morning off to help get yourself together, physically and mentally, to prepare to return to work.

Perhaps, your company offers flex time as a work schedule option. Your typical work hours are 8:00 AM to 4:30 PM, but you can come into work at 6:00 AM in order to get off at 2:30 PM so you can catch an afternoon flight. Conversely, instead of coming in at 8:00 AM, you have the option to come in at 10:00 AM and leave work at 6:30 PM so you can have those couple of hours Monday morning to collect yourself upon returning from a trip the previous weekend. Tip number four is to take advantage of flex time if it is available to you.

5. Seasons – Weather/Climate

There are three seasons you must consider. The first two seasons pertain to the weather/climate. Before we get into discussing these seasons, let's do a brief overview on weather and climate.

According to NASA, "weather is basically the way the atmosphere is behaving, mainly with respect to its effects upon life and human activities. The difference between weather and climate is that weather consists of the short-term (minutes to months) changes in the atmosphere;"[16] whereas, climate refers to a long-term, usually thirty-year pattern of weather in a particular area. In other words, "an easy way to remember the difference is that climate is what you expect, like a very hot summer, and weather is what you get, like a hot day with pop-up thunderstorms."[17]   While it would be awesome to be able to know for certain what the weather will be like months from now as we are presently planning for our vacation, it's simply not possible. No one can predict with 100 percent accuracy and precision that far in advance, but what we can do is review scientific data comprised of "averages of precipitation, temperature, humidity, sunshine, wind velocity, phenomena such as fog, frost, and hail storms, and other measures of the weather that occur over a long period in a particular place,"[18] otherwise known as the climate. So, that is what we shall do. With that said, let's continue with the discussion of the first type of season to consider when planning your trip.

For the most part, every region of the world has a time of the year deemed the rainy season in which there are significant amounts of rainfall. If you are scheduling a trip where you plan to be outdoors the majority of the time, whether you are in a park exploring nature or sightseeing in the city, you may want to

---

[16] Dunbar, "What's the Difference?"
[17] Ibid.
[18] Ibid.

avoid traveling to your destination during this time. On the flipside of this, prices are often quite cheaper during the rainy season because tourism is commonly down during this time. Flight and hotel prices are frequently lower as opposed to other times of the year when rain is no issue. If you are planning a trip where you intend on being inside for the majority of your stay, perhaps the rain is not a factor for you. If this is the case, you may want to book your trip during that time of the year to take advantage of the inexpensive associated cost.

Also related to weather/climate, you must be aware of the seasons – spring, summer, fall, and winter – in your destination location. Just because it is summer in July in your home location does not mean that it is warm and sunny in July where you plan to visit. You should look at a climate map or historical temperature data for your proposed destination to identify months of the year when there are extreme temperatures versus average temperatures so that you can plan your travel accordingly. It is no fun being outdoors in 110° F weather or -40° F weather if that is not the type of environment you had in mind for your vacation. In order to research the rainy season, climate, and average temperatures for an area, you can normally do a quick internet search for those terms paired with the name of the place you want to visit.

6. Tourism Cycle and Busy Season

The third season you must consider pertains to the tourism cycle. In several locations, there is what is considered a busy season. This is the time of year when there tends to be a lot of scheduled events, activities, and attractions. This may consist of an annual festival, concert series, local holiday festivities, or it just may be a popular time of year for travelers because the weather is favorable.

During the busy season, prices are usually higher. This is an opportunity for businesses to maximize their revenues. Not only is there a peak in transportation and lodging prices, but parking, venue, food, entertainment, and keepsake prices are also noticeably increased. If you desire to visit a location specifically to attend a popular event or activity, this is fine. You just need to make sure you plan well in advance so that you have an opportunity to take advantage of the best pricing and availability in terms of transportation and lodging. Whether you are flying, taking the bus, or renting a car to drive and staying in a hotel, Airbnb, or hostel, you must plan ahead because for some extremely popular annual events, arrangements must be made over a year ahead of time. Do your research.

Generally speaking, lodging near the event is more expensive. So, if you want to save money on lodging, you can stay somewhere on the other side of town or just outside of town and take public transportation or utilize a rideshare service to get to and from the event. If you prefer not to skimp on the place to stay, you can lodge near the venue of the event and walk to and from the event and save money on transportation as long as the area is pedestrian friendly. If money is not a concern for you, you may want to pay to stay near the venue and pay for transportation as well. The key take-away here is that the busy season may impact the time of year you visit a location and how much the trip will cost you, so plan with this information in mind.

Many years ago, I was interested in attending the Albuquerque International Balloon Fiesta. At the time, I had never been to New Mexico and thought it would be a fun activity to center my trip around as I explored the city and nearby areas. Drawing approximately a million people annually in recent years, this event takes place for about nine days in the beginning of October. I figured it'd be cool to see a bunch of hot air balloons ascending simultaneously and even get the chance to ride in one.

When I looked at hotel prices during the festival plus a few days before and after, they were more than double the cost of a stay a couple weeks before or after the event. While I was initially enamored by the idea of the glorious fiesta, I recognized rather quickly that this tourist attraction was a major revenue generator for the city and would cost me a lot more than I was willing to pay for the experience.

So, I ended up visiting New Mexico the following July, enjoying a relaxing summer vacation in Albuquerque and Santa Fe. During my time there, I was able to view a handful of hot air balloons as I delighted in my very own sunrise flight. Sure, it was no Albuquerque International Balloon Fiesta, but I was highly satisfied with my trip, and I was able to spend the money I saved by visiting the area outside busy season towards another trip. So, I was blessed with two vacations for the price of one.

7. Currency

When considering international travel, it is good to know what type of currency is used at your potential travel destination and the exchange rate between that currency and the currency where you live. This is important because it will essentially let you know how much your money is "worth" and how far it will go. I learned this invaluable lesson during the summer I interned in Europe.

As an undergraduate, I was working for an American organization at a job based in Germany. Given my spirit of wanderlust, when I wasn't working, I used my downtime to explore Europe. For my birthday weekend in July, two of my fellow interns and I decided that we would spend our four-day

Independence Day holiday weekend in Spain. We got a great deal that included bus transportation, individual four-star hotel room, daily breakfast buffet, and an excursion to Barcelona from Lloret de Mar for about $260 USD. In order to have money to spend on food, entertainment, activities, and souvenirs, prior to the trip, I went to the bank and exchanged $200 in USD to Spanish pesetas (abbreviated ESP – the currency in Spain at that time). That ended up being more than enough money for those four days, and I *thoroughly* enjoyed myself considering that I was celebrating my 21st birthday.

Fast-forward a few weeks to the three-day weekend trip I took to London with one of my other intern colleagues. Like I had done before for my trip to Spain, I had gone to the bank to exchange $200 USD. It had worked well for me before, so I figured I would do it again. By our second day in London, I had run out of cash and was frantically searching for an ATM to get more money. Why was this? Did I splurge and "ball out of control"? No, in fact, it was just the opposite. I was very conservative with my spending in comparison to my trip in Spain because I was noticing how it seemed like everything was costing me so much more.

The primary difference was the conversion rate and the "value" of the money. At the time of my Spain trip, the exchange rate was about 1 USD to 163 ESP, whereas, when I was in London, the exchange rate for British pounds (abbreviated GBP) was about 1 GBP to 1.57 USD. You may be thinking, "Well, if 1 GBP equals 1.57 USD, wouldn't that just mean that the GBP prices would simply be lower to be about as much as what you would pay in USD?" No, that is not necessarily how it works. Just because something in America may cost you $1.57 does not mean that it would be priced at 1 GBP in London at that time. It may be priced at 2 GBP, which means you would be paying the equivalent of $3.14 USD. This means that your money would not stretch as far, and this is what happened to me. So, I am explaining all of this to emphasize that you must be aware of the exchange rate between the currency of the country you are considering visiting and the currency of your country of residence.

There are quite a few currency converters available online and via smartphone or tablet. Before and during travel, I tend to use the XE Currency app on my phone. I downloaded it for free several years ago and have found it to be very convenient and user-friendly. It is available at the Apple App Store and Google Play Store and includes a calculator and historical exchange rate charts. In addition to XE Currency, Travel Savvy recommends CalConvert, Currency Convert, and My Currency Converter & Rates for Apple users and rounds out their list of the five best currency converter apps of this present year with Valuta+ which is available via Google Play. CalConvert not only provides currency conversion but also converts hundreds of other units, and it includes a calculator with scientific and mathematical functions. If you trade in virtual currency, Currency Convert will benefit you in that it supports BitCoin, DogeCoin, and more. My Currency Converter & Rates supplies a basic calculator and historical exchange rates. Valuta+ is the simplest as it strictly converts currency. All of these apps render free versions, and most can be run offline.

8. Budget

"You don't have to be rich to travel well."

– Eugene Fodor

Now that we have discussed currency, let's continue the conversation on money. It is a "no-brainer" that your budget is a huge factor as you plan where and when you plan to travel. There are two main ways you can view your budget when organizing a trip. The first perspective is to think about how much money you are willing to spend or have available to spend and let that dictate where you will go based on the estimated cost of the trips you are deliberating over. The other way to look at it would be to determine where it is that you want to go, find out how much it will cost, and devise a method to pay for it. Following the former strategy causes the size of your budget to lead you to your choices of destinations. In the latter approach, you select your destination and in doing so, it will lead to establishing/securing your budget.

By going with the first strategy, you are being fiscally responsible by living within your means and limiting debt increase, which has multiple benefits. You are able to enjoy your time away without paying for it (literally and figuratively) when you get back. You may be able to go on the trip sooner than you would if you were to select the second strategy. It is possible that you may be able to go on more than one trip, since the trips within your budget may be less expensive. A drawback from choosing the first strategy is that the destinations that are currently within your budget may not be at the top of your list of dream destinations, so you may feel like you would be settling a bit by visiting those locations.

If you follow the second strategy, you have a considerable degree of flexibility. The obvious benefit is that you get to go where you really want to go. In contrast to the previous scenario, you are, in fact, focused on locations at the top of your list of dream destinations. A possible con of going with this option is that you may not be able to go on the trip as soon as you would like because you don't have enough money now, so you have to save up for it. The good thing, though, is that you are able to go. This is where the flexibility enters. You can take as long as you need to take to set aside the money you need. You can work overtime or extra shifts or bring in more cashflow from additional income streams. Alternatively or additionally, you can reduce your spending by cutting back on paying for things that may not be a true necessity like frequent dining out and entertainment or multiple cable/streaming services. If you do select the second strategy, the key is to be financially responsible. Don't spend money on a trip that you can't really afford especially if your primary motive is to try to impress people. Trust me – it is not worth it. I acknowledge that it takes patience and discipline to stick to a budget, but it is the right thing to do.

Putting the Pieces Together

Now, the real fun begins! You get to take all the information you have learned thus far and apply it in order to help you make some practical decisions. Follow these steps to help you determine your travel destination(s) and when you should go.

1. Brainstorm a list of all the possible places you may want to go. Think about incredible pictures you have seen on people's Instagram or Facebook pages, travel shows or commercials you may have viewed that displayed beautiful scenery of a specific place, or stories you have heard about amazing experiences people have had in

particular places. Begin generating the list on a sheet of paper or inserting them into the column of a spreadsheet. I, personally, prefer the spreadsheet because it is organized, and it makes it a lot easier and cleaner to edit as you go through the various steps of this process.

2. Next, what you will do is gather basic information about each of the locations on your list pertaining to the factors of culture, travel documents, vaccinations/ immunizations, currency, and budget. At this point, you are not striving to become an expert in each location. You are just doing some "quick and dirty" research to help you weed out locations that are not a good fit for you and prioritize the locations that remain on your list. As a guide, seek to find answers to the following questions and utilize the tips.

   A. Culture

      1. Language

      Questions:

- What language do they speak in the location?

- Is it a language you know or one with which you have some familiarity?

- If not, would you feel comfortable in that environment not knowing or being familiar with the language?

Tips: For information about language, you can reference the nation's BBC Country Profile or The World Factbook's One-Page Summary. Remember, in areas where there is a lot of tourism, meaning that people visit from all over the world, there is a strong possibility that the natives speak and understand at least some basic English. So, try not to let yourself get too stressed out about not knowing the language. As I mentioned before, it is good to know some keywords and common phrases, but there is no need to be fluent.

2. Religion, Politics, Ethnicity, and Social Beliefs

   Questions:

   - Based on the country's religious, political, and social beliefs, would you feel comfortable in the environment?

   - Do you think your safety and/or security may be compromised in any way?

   - Is it possible that your ethnicity may garner stares, pointing, unflattering comments and/or questions?

- If so, would that make you feel uncomfortable to the point that you may not want to visit the area?

Tips: The World Factbook, BBC Country Profiles, U.S. Department of State Travel Country Information and Traveler Information, and category-specific Facebook groups are excellent resources for retrieving information about these topics. Remember to base your decisions on facts and not the opinions of family members, friends, or associates who have not been to the location. If when you research a place via the Department of State's website, you learn that the location is unsafe for American travelers, this is an obvious red flag. For example, in the Safety and Security section in the Country Information for Libya, the website currently states: "The Department of State advises U.S. citizens against all travel to Libya, as the security situation in Libya remains unpredictable and unstable." It goes on to warn against travel due to terrorist threats, kidnapping, and violence. To put it another way, this place is off limits. Additionally, if you feel you may not be able to adapt to a particular area or the environment may be unsafe for you personally, remove the location from your list. There is nothing wrong with doing this. Go by your gut. It is better to be safe than sorry.

B. Travel Documents

Questions:

- What travel documents are needed for you to enter the location?

- Do you currently possess the needed documents?

- If not, roughly how long would it take for you to acquire the documents?

Tips: The questions for this section are not geared towards determining whether or not you will visit a particular location but, rather, the timing of the anticipated visit. For instance, if the place you are interested in traveling to requires you to have a passport and a visa and you have neither, you will be able to go to this place, just not within the next couple of weeks. For information related to travel documents, check out the country's One-Page Summary in The World Factbook and/or the website of the U.S. Department of State – Bureau of Consular Affairs at www.travel.state.gov.

C. Vaccinations/Immunizations

Questions:

- Are any vaccinations/immunizations required or recommended to enter the location?

- If so, how quickly can you receive them?

Tips: Similar to the section on travel documents, the questions in this section are not designed to help you figure out whether or not you are going to a particular location but, instead, when you would be available to go to said location. If you need a vaccination, but you are not able to get an appointment to see your doctor until a few months down the line or get a vaccination from a clinic within a few days or weeks, you would need to account for the appropriate amount of time for this as you plan your trip. For basic information about required/recommended vaccinations, take a look at the Quick Facts section of Country Information within the International Travel section of the U.S. Department of State Travel website or the Travel Facts by country within the World Factbook provided by the CIA. For more detailed information regarding required/suggested vaccinations and medications broken down by region and environment, visit the website of the Centers for Disease Control (CDC) and Prevention and search by destination under the Traveler's Health section.

D. Time Available

Questions:

- Given the length of time you anticipate that you desire to spend in the location, do you have time readily available?

- If not, what adjustments are needed in order to get the time, and approximately how long would it take?

Tips: For this category, you are essentially checking how much vacation time or PTO you have available as well as upcoming holidays. You also want to review your schedule to refresh your memory of any business or personal engagements to which you have already committed to avoid conflicts.

E. Currency

Question:

- Is the exchange rate favorable, unfavorable, or neutral?

Tips: Use a currency converter like the XE Currency app to find out the exchange rate between the currency used at your potential travel destination and the currency where you live. If your money will not go far based on the exchange rate of the destination currency, then this would be considered unfavorable. If the exchange rate has your money comparable to the value of your home country's currency, this would be deemed neutral. Lastly, if the exchange rate is such that the value of the destination currency allows you to spend a little and receive a lot in return, this is wonderful (i.e., favorable). Enjoy your trip!

F. Budget

Questions:

- According to the estimated cost of the trip, do you have money available now to take the trip?

- If not, about how long would it take for you to be able to afford the trip? A month or less? Five months or less? More than five months?

Tips: Coupling the data you collected related to currency with a ballpark figure of anticipated expenses (i.e., transportation, lodging, food, and entertainment), assess a roundabout cost for the trip. Compare that dollar amount with the amount of money you currently have saved. Only you know your personal financial situation. Plan within your means.

1. Use this information to begin eliminating destinations from your list and rearranging the order of the destinations that remain based on how they align with the factors you have considered so far. That is to say, at the top of your list should be destinations where you have no cultural concerns, you have the necessary travel documents in-hand, you presently meet the vaccination/immunization requirements, and you have plenty of time and money available for the trip now. These we will refer to as your Tier One travel destinations. Just below these destinations should be those that may involve some minor adapting to the culture, waiting on documents or vaccinations/immunizations, adjusting of your schedule, and/or saving of money. These are your Tier Two travel destinations. Last and least, are your Tier Three travel destinations, which may require a considerable amount of adapting, waiting, adjusting, and/or saving. Focus on your Tier One and Tier Two travel destinations, as they will be easier and quicker to start planning for immediately. The Tier Three travel destinations should either be moved to the very bottom of your list or removed from the list entirely.

2. For your Tier One and Tier Two travel destinations, research data about the seasons – winter, spring, summer, fall, rainy, and busy. Ascertain the best months to travel to each based on the seasons.

Homing in on Your Travel Dates and Destinations

There are two different strategies for helping you try to narrow down your travel dates and destination(s).

1. If you don't have much time available to travel, look at your list of Tier One destinations and figure out which ones you can travel to in the amount of time you have available.

2. If time availability is not a big concern:

    a. If you are interested in planning a multi-city trip, focus on grouping destinations with close geographical proximity that have overlapping best months to travel.

    b. Based on today's date, look at planning trips during months that are relatively close to the current date but allow enough time for you to plan adequately and remain within your budget.

Use your list of potential travel destinations with best months to travel along with your length of availability to select specific dates on your calendar. Now that you know where you are going and when, you are ready to proceed to Step Two: Decide How to Get There and How to Get around While There.

STEP TWO – Decide How to Get There and How to Get around While There

> *"Enjoy the journey as much as the destination."*
> *– Marshall Sylver*

So, now that you know where and when you are going, it's time to determine how you are going to get there and how you are going to get around while you're there. A few key factors to acknowledge when trying to decide your mode of transportation are the location of the destination, cost, travel duration, amount of time available for travel, and comfort level. Take these into account as you explore your options.

How to Get There

Cruises

A cruise is an excellent option for a first-time solo traveler, someone who is planning his/her own trip for the first time, or somebody who appreciates the convenience of one-stop shopping. Though you may be taking the trip by yourself, you are certainly never "alone" on a cruise. For those who have shied away from solo travel out of fear or uneasiness of being alone, a cruise allows you to be in a group where you can mingle with others or be to yourself as you please. There is also a unique sense of safety and security in numbers on a ship versus wandering through the streets of a new foreign city by yourself. For those who are new to planning and organizing trips, a cruise is a dream because a lot of the planning and organizing is done for you. Transportation to and from your destinations, excursions, lodging arrangements, entertainment, activities, and even dinner plans are pretty much taken care of when you book a cruise. It is basically a brilliantly packaged deal wrapped up with a bow on top. All you simply have to do is select the best cruise for yourself, and I've got a plethora of information to share with you to assist with that process.

Guidance for Selecting a Cruise

For a cruise to be considered as one of your transportation options, your travel destination has to have a port to which cruise lines sail. There are over five hundred ports sailed by cruises worldwide, so there is a strong possibility that your destination is among the list or in a nearby location. You can find out by doing a simple internet search for your destination plus the word *cruise*. If there are, in fact, cruises to your destination, the search results should reveal some of the cruise lines that sail to your destination. One thing you will want to pay attention to is the embarkation port – where you would board the ship for departure. You need to decide if you mind flying to a departure point or if you would rather only leave from a departure point that is within a reasonable driving distance. This is important because it will impact the budget for your trip. If you have to fly to the departure point, you need to factor in the cost of the roundtrip flight on top of what you will be paying for the cruise.

Most Americans live within driving distance (up to seven hours) of a cruise port that ships depart from, which is known as a homeport. United States homeports exist in these states:[19]

- Alabama

- California

- Florida

- Hawaii

- Louisiana

- Maryland

---

[19] Cruise Critic Staff, "Choose a Cruise."

- Massachusetts

- New Jersey

- New York

- South Carolina

- Texas

- Virginia

- Washington

Bear in mind that cruise ships might not depart from every homeport year-round.[20]

Europeans looking to cruise may also find homeports that are within driving distance from themselves. In the United Kingdom, ships depart from Dover, Greenock, Liverpool, London, and Southampton. Some other European homeports for cruises on the ocean are as follows:[21]

- Amsterdam, Netherlands

- Athens, Greece

- Barcelona, Spain

- Copenhagen, Denmark

---

[20] Ibid.
[21] Ibid.

- Venice, Italy

In Australia, the majority of the cruise ships sail from Sydney, but some departures are also available from Adelaide, Brisbane, Fremantle (Perth), and Melbourne.[22]

With regard to South America, you can depart from multiple port cities in Brazil:

- Bahia de Salvador

- Maceio

- Manaus

- Rio de Janeiro

- Santos (Sao Paulo)

There are also ports in the following locations:

- Buenos Aires and Ushuaia, Argentina

- Santiago, San Antonio, and Valparaiso, Chile

- Callao (Lima) and Lima, Peru

- Montevideo, Uruguay

Homeports in Africa consist of those in Cairo, Egypt; Cape Town and Durban, South Africa; and Dakar, Senegal.

---

[22] Ibid.

In Asia and the Middle East, there are several homeports:

- Singapore

- Hong Kong

- Philippines

- Japan

- Cambodia

- Vietnam

- Indonesia

- Thailand

- Myanmar

- Laos

- Sri Lanka

- Maldives

- India

- Taiwan

- Malaysia

- Turkey

- United Arab Emirates

- Qatar

- Jordan

- Israel

Many of these international homeports in Europe, Australia, South America, Africa, and Asia are also port stops on cruises. So, if you're interested in doing a cruise abroad, you may want to look into some of these locations. Several cruise companies offer deals that conjoin flights and accommodations for cruises departing internationally.[23]

Once you identify which departure points you are willing to consider that sail to your dream destination, that will begin to narrow down some of your options in terms of cruise lines and cruise ships. Travel dates and cruise length will help you further filter your list of choices.

In Step One, when choosing the best months to travel, we used winter, spring, summer, fall, rainy, and busy seasons as factors. When you are seeking to go on a cruise, one more season you must factor in is hurricane season. The Caribbean and Mediterranean are the most popular cruise destinations and can be sailed year-round; however, Caribbean itineraries can be altered by hurricanes from June through October.[24] If you have your heart set on visiting a Caribbean location during hurricane

---

[23] TravelOnline, "Know Before You Go Cruising."
[24] Cruise Critic Staff.

season, perhaps, you may consider flying there directly and staying at a resort versus taking a cruise, as it could be a little safer. That is not to say that the island itself would be undisturbed, so you would still be required to exercise caution.

Though there are many cruise destinations available for year-round sailing, there are some itineraries that can only be sailed during particular times of the year. Alaska is a prime example, as a great majority of Alaskan cruises occur from May to September with a handful encompassing late April and early October, and those solely include southern Alaskan ports.[25]

Similarly, cruises to Antarctica are mostly available from October to March, and Arctic cruises typically run from April through September. When I booked my cruise to Antarctica, I chose to go in December because it was somewhat "warmer" compared to other months, since December in Antarctica is actually during the summer. Furthermore, I knew that the temperatures impact the type of sea life (e.g., penguins, whales, seals) I'd get to see and activities I would be able to participate in (e.g., kayaking, hiking, camping). I figured this would be a once-in-a-lifetime trip, so I wanted to make sure I experienced all that I desired. With that said, I reiterate that it is important to

---

[25] Ibid.

always reflect on the purpose of your trip when making defining decisions.

The length of the cruise paired with the amount of time you have available for your trip will help you further narrow down your selections. Durations can range anywhere from two nights to two hundred-plus days on a world cruise. If you don't have much time available for your trip, you can seek out three-to-four-night weekend itineraries. The average cruise sailings span from five to fourteen nights.[26]

At this point, you should have a fairly decent list of potential cruise lines and ships for your trip based on your travel destination, embarkation port, travel dates, and cruise length. From here, your decision will likely be influenced by your personal preference and fit, interests, and budget.

Perhaps, you are planning to go on your first cruise and are a bit apprehensive. *Cruise Critic* published a list in March 2020 of some of the best cruises for first-timers. Here are a few from the list relevant to solo travelers along with a description of the type of traveler to which the cruise line ordinarily appeals.[27]

- Carnival Cruise Line and Norwegian Cruise Line (NCL) are deemed best for value hunters. Both lines have

---

[26] Ibid.
[27] Cruise Critic, "Cruises for First Timers."

sizable fleets with ample passenger capacity and offer access to popular destinations with various options for itineraries, which translates to low prices and frequent deals. Carnival's cruises normally start around $80 USD per person, per night and can be seized for even less with promotional fares. With NCL's frequent last-minute deals, one can obtain rates as low as $50 or $75 USD per person, per night. Both cruise lines also grant access to a variety of on-board complimentary dining venues and numerous free activities like listening and dancing to live music and attending Broadway shows and comedy shows.

- Regent Seven Seas Cruises and Seabourn are suggested cruise lines for luxury seekers. These lines have ships with gorgeous, spacious all-suite cabins starting at around three hundred square feet, superb service, and a huge variety of dining options, drinks, and entertainment all included along with gratuities. Regent Seven Seas, arguably the most inclusive of the biggest luxury brands, also includes in its fares pre- and post-cruise tours and hotel stays, and shore excursions. In addition, they have the highest staff-to-passenger ratios in the industry. Whether it be the butler in the penthouse suite aboard a Regent Seven Seas ship or the vast spas and bath drawn by the cabin steward, complete with strewn flower petals and aromatherapy scents on a Seabourn ship, these cruise lines truly know how to pamper their guests.

- Silversea Cruises and Holland America Line are recommended as the best for mature cruisers. Silversea rarely has children on-board and its all-inclusive upfront fares with room service, wine and spirits, gratuities, and transportation into town from port appeal to seasoned travelers. Holland has traditionally attracted a more mature crowd by accentuating "the classic cruising experience over partying and pushing the adrenaline limits."[28] They present quieter pleasures such as cooking demonstrations and hands-on workshops, self-guided art tours of the on-board art collections, and special on-board talks that strive to highlight local culture and history. Also, they provide low impact athletic activities like tai chi and yoga as well as tennis. Silversea's nine small ships that accommodate merely one hundred to 596 guests each are well-suited for guests searching for easy camaraderie, as well as for those with limited mobility. Additionally, they have itineraries spanning eight hundred-plus locales across all seven continents

---

[28] Ibid.

which caters to seasoned travelers seeking to explore new horizons.

- Appearing previously on the list, Holland America Line and Norwegian Cruise Line are also popular lines for singles. Holland America draws solo travelers with its Single Partners Program comprised of hosted parties for on-board singles early on in the cruise and special singles-themed cocktail parties and games, which allow solo cruisers sufficient time to mingle. Moreover, upon request, the line will group singles together for dining. Prior to the trip, they facilitate a roommate matching service with fellow solo travelers of the same gender, and if they are unable to facilitate an adequate pairing for a participant, that person is guaranteed a double occupancy fare. This is a big deal because one would normally otherwise have to pay a single supplement, which can be pricey. As an alternate, Holland America has a couple of ships in its fleet with dedicated single cabins. In a similar way, NCL caught the attention of solo cruisers when it introduced the Studio concept that has cabins with stylish minimalist furnishings and no single supplement. Cruisers who book this category of cabin receive private access to a lounge with a bar, snacks, and space for socializing, too.

- Oceania Cruises and Seabourn are known as the best cruise lines for foodies. This is primarily because Oceania has famous French chef Jacques Pepin as its executive culinary director, while Seabourn has a culinary partnership with lauded American chef Thomas Keller, renowned for his multiple Michelin-starred eateries. Oceania's main dining rooms provide high-quality cuisine in an open-seating plan, and even their buffets and poolside grill fare fail to disappoint. "Lobsters come sourced from the line's own Maine lobster farm, and its beef is dry-aged for 28 days in Oceania's aging facility. Specialty venues are fee-free (minus special wine-pairing menus) and range from the Asian-style Red Ginger to Italian Toscana and French bistro Jacques."[29] Seabourn's chef conveys his "unique brand of French-American fare that is infused with regional flavors."[30]

- Norwegian Cruise Line and Royal Caribbean International were chosen as best for entertainment enthusiasts. Every Norwegian ship offers musical revues, comedy and improv shows, live music, and guest performers. NCL and Royal Caribbean both have

---

[29] Ibid.
[30] Ibid.

Broadway musicals like *Jersey Boys*, *Rock of Ages*, and *After Midnight*. Also, there is *Million Dollar Quartet* with Norwegian and *Grease* and *Mamma Mia!* with Royal Caribbean. Royal Caribbean, however, takes performances outside of the theater with "ice-skating shows in on-board rinks, high-diving acrobatic shows at the pool-based AquaTheater and aerial shows in ship atriums."[31] NCL also has music by dueling pianists and blues bands, its dinner theater show Cirque Dreams, bars, discos, bowling, and Wii for entertainment.

Since budget is one of the focuses of this book, I would be remiss if I did not provide one more list: *U.S. News & World Report's* Best Cruise Lines for the Money in 2020. U.S. News ranked the cruise lines according to a "methodology that factors in itinerary affordability, health ratings, and reputation among experts and travelers." The list includes companies based in North America and Europe with Caribbean, European, and Alaskan destinations.[32]

1. Royal Caribbean International

2. Celebrity Cruises

3. Norwegian Cruise Line

---

[31] Ibid.
[32] U.S. News & World Report, "Cruise Lines for Money."

4. Princess Cruises

5. Carnival Cruise Line

6. Holland America Line

7. MSC Cruises

8. Costa Cruises (a member of the Carnival family)

Hacks for Saving Money

Continuing with the theme of budget, here are some ways you can save money on cruises with Carnival and Royal Caribbean as well as cruises in general.

Before You Book the Cruise

1. Search for deals on the various cruise line websites. At carnival.com under the *Today's Deals* section, you can often find their latest deals and very low last-minute offers.[33] From the royalcaribbean.com homepage, check out Royal Deals. Sporadically, there is an offer of free gratuities or specialty dining. Throughout the year, Royal Caribbean holds sales that include fare reductions and perks like shipboard credit that can be used for drinks and other expenses.[34] Norwegian Cruise Line also extends shipboard credit offers, so be sure to seek them

---

[33] Golden, "Save on Carnival Cruise."
[34] Golden, "Save on Royal Caribbean."

out on their website if interested.[35] If it will be awhile before you book your trip, you may want to sign up for emailed deal alerts from the various cruise lines that provide them.[36] Perhaps, you're already locked in on your dates for travel and there is a lengthy amount of time before your anticipated trip. Occasionally, you can get a really good deal by booking your reservation several months in advance. When I was looking into cruise lines for my trip to Antarctica, I came across an offer allowing me to save nearly 17 percent off by booking my reservation by the end of February for my trip in December. I was excited to take advantage of that tremendous savings!

2. Find out if you qualify for special discounts. Some lines supply discounts to members of the United States military, police department, or fire department. There may also be senior discounts for travelers ages fifty-five and older.[37]

3. Choose to leave from a port to which you can drive. As aforementioned, there are several homeports. You save money by leaving from a port you can drive to versus

---

[35] Golden, "Save on Carnival Cruise."
[36] Golden, "Save on Royal Caribbean."
[37] Ibid.

one to which you have to fly. Additionally, if you do drive, utilize off-site parking because it is less expensive than parking at the pier.[38]

4. Sail on one of the cruise line's older ships. While the latest and greatest ships have all the newest attractions, many of the ships just a few years older still have fun and thrilling activities but at bargain prices.[39]

5. Consider downgrading your cabin type. Cruise ships have a variety of cabin categories to choose from, and each is sold at a different price point. For instance, an inside cabin without a window is significantly cheaper than a suite. Think about how much time you plan on spending in your cabin versus being out and about on the ship taking advantage of the activities, entertainment, dining, and socializing, and let that factor into your cabin selection decision. You might find that you can "afford" to downgrade your cabin category and save money.[40]

6. If you will be cruising with Carnival and are somewhat of a risk taker, ponder purchasing a guarantee rate cabin. Guarantee cabins are cabins specially priced below the

---

[38] Ibid.
[39] Ibid.
[40] Cruise Critic Staff.

regular cruise rate. The catch is that in exchange for this low rate, you do not get to pick a specific cabin but instead, the cruise line will decide what level of cabin you will get based on availability. It is a bit of a gamble, but who knows? You may luck out and choose a guarantee interior cabin that sells out, allowing you to be upgraded to a cabin with a view. Nevertheless, on the flipside, you may wind up in an interior cabin in a less sought-after section of the ship. If it doesn't really matter to you where you sleep, selecting a guarantee rate cabin would be an easy way for you to save some cash.[41]

7. If you are in the market for a credit card and know that you will likely be taking multiple trips via cruise, you can sign up for a cruise line credit card. Carnival's free credit card called the Carnival World Mastercard allows cardholders to earn points for every dollar they spend, which can, in turn, be redeemed for merchandise, on-board amenities, or a statement credit.[42] Likewise, Royal Caribbean's branded Visa credit card lets cardholders earn points they can use for on-board credit. You may be able to take advantage of a welcome deal where you sign up for the card and get ten thousand bonus points if

---

[41] Golden, "Save on Carnival Cruise."
[42] Ibid.

you use the card to make a purchase within the first ninety days. Those points can be cashed in for $100 USD in on-board credit.[43]

8. Before your first Carnival cruise, join the Very Important Fun Person (VIFP) Club, where you can gain access to special cruise deals like 30 percent off during an end-of-summer sale. You can also take advantage of early saver savings, up to 25 percent off, when itineraries are first announced. Starting on your second sailing, you can get on-board perks such as a large bottle of water at no cost. As you proceed up the five tiers by earning points for each Carnival cruise, the perks get better such as attaining cabin upgrades.[44]

Before Going on the Cruise

1. Bid on an upgraded cabin. With Royal Caribbean, once patrons have booked their cruise, select cruisers are invited to go online and bid for a cabin upgrade. Repeat cruisers or those signed up for the marketing emails from the line have a higher probability of receiving an invitation. If you were to receive an invitation, your participation would be voluntary and free, and you would decide how much you want to bid. You only pay

[43] Golden, "Save on Royal Caribbean."
[44] Golden, "Save on Carnival Cruise."

if your bid is accepted. It's worth a shot at getting a fancier room at a bargain price.[45]

2. Purchase an internet plan with the cruise line or international mobile plan through your cell phone provider. Obviously, you can save the most amount of money by going off the grid altogether and having an unplugged vacation; however, if you do want to have Wi-Fi access and remain connected on your social media, you can save by booking your internet plan in advance versus buying it once on-board at a higher rate. Alternatively, review the phone and data plans carried by your service provider to compare rates, as you want to make sure you are getting the best deal.

3. Bring some drinks and/or buy a drink package. The beverage allowance varies per cruise line in terms of the quantity of bottles or cans of alcoholic or non-alcoholic beverages you can bring on-board, so find out what the policy is for the line you choose. If you are not traveling with a luxury line where most, if not all, your drinks are included, you may have to pay for bottled water, soda, juice, beer, wine, champagne, and alcoholic and non-alcoholic cocktails. If you are a large consumer of any of

---

[45] Golden, "Save on Royal Caribbean."

these products, it would behoove you to purchase the corresponding drink package in advance of your cruise in order to save money. Otherwise, prices are a lot higher if you order on-board.[46]

4. Think about ordering a specialty dining package pre-cruise. You may be able to save up to 40 percent if you book the plan ahead of time.[47]

5. Pre-book your shore excursions. You may achieve discounts of five to 25 percent or more by not waiting to purchase on-board.[48]

6. If you know in advance that you want to purchase the photos taken by the cruise line photographers, sign up for a photo package pre-cruise if it is available. Carnival offers a package that allows you to save 37 percent if you buy it before the cruise.[49]

7. If you will be on a cruise for days, I advise you to pack plenty of clothes so that you do not need to pay for laundry services during your cruise. If, however, your itinerary is over a period of weeks or months and you

---

[46] Ibid.
[47] Ibid.
[48] Ibid.
[49] Golden, "Save on Carnival Cruise."

will need to utilize laundry services, look out for laundry specials while on-board.[50]

During the Cruise

1. Stick to the free dining options if you did not order a specialty dining package. Also, avoid the fee-based treats and premium coffee. There are usually complimentary alternatives like the self-serve, soft-serve ice cream and self-serve coffee.[51]

2. Delay your souvenir purchases. Before paying full price for the T-shirts and knick-knacks in the shipboard shops on the first day of your cruise, be aware that there will be sales throughout the cruise, especially in the latter part. An even better option would be to purchase souvenirs onshore from the locals. The deals will be even better, plus you will be contributing to the community.[52]

3. If near the end of your cruise, you know that you want to plan another cruise in the near future, contemplate going on and booking your next trip while on the ship, as you will save money. If you need a little time to think about it, ask questions about when the deals expire.

---

[50] Golden, "Save on Royal Caribbean."
[51] Ibid.
[52] Golden, "Save on Carnival Cruise."

Sometimes, you can still take advantage of the sales up to four weeks post-cruise.[53]

Booking the Cruise

If you have narrowed down which cruise line you want to sail with, you can book with them directly via website or phone, as they can offer you some of the best pricing and answer any questions you may have. If you are not interested in a particular line or are seeking to explore your options, you can check out some of the common travel search engines that you would typically use to book flights, hotels, or rental cars.

Expedia, who owns Travelocity and Orbitz, provides an excellent platform for searching for cruises. Though the pricing may be similar to some of the deals you find on the cruise line sites, an added benefit is their ability to offer packages that couple the cruise with lodging at a pre-departure hotel, potentially saving you even more money. The Priceline website not only permits you to compare prices of numerous cruise lines at once but also presents deals exclusive to Priceline with bonus amenities like $1,000 in on-board credit and $50 USD off shore

---

[53] Ibid.

excursions. Kayak is another popular travel search engine that can yield several options for cruise deals.[54]

CheapCaribbean.com, CruiseDirect, and Cruisewatch have sites specifically dedicated to searching for cruises. While the CheapCaribbean.com name would lead you to believe that it is focused on Caribbean cruises only, it actually compares all over the world. One of their major incentives is that they offer a cruise loyalty club that can be combined with any cruise line's loyalty program as well as appealing perks such as no money down to book, on-board credit, free cocktails for the duration of your cruise, spa credit, and cash back on your booking. These perks vary per cruise, but you can normally get at least one of these bonuses.

CruiseDirect has served over five hundred thousand travelers globally and boasts an A+ Better Business Bureau rating. In addition, they offer bonuses on most sailings, such as on-board credit or free items like drinks, Wi-Fi, gratuities, travel insurance, or specialty dining experience.

Not your ordinary cruise booking website, Cruisewatch proclaims to be a "digital cruise advisor" that pairs data power with personalization. It uses artificial intelligence to help you efficiently search and book cruises, which is pretty impressive.

---

[54] Andrews, "Book Your Cruise."

Nevertheless, an even more remarkable feat is its capability to use its comprehensive price history to predict cruise prices and drops with an accuracy rate of around 80 percent! Utilizing the Cruisewatch site's cruise price prediction alerts, travelers are able to save up to 70 percent by merely booking at the right time.[55]

With this extensive bit of information you have received about cruises, you should experience "smooth sailing" as you make your travel plans. Bon voyage!

Plane Flights

Flying is normally the form of transportation that can get you to your destination the quickest, but it can also be the most expensive route if you don't shop around for deals. The good news is that there is an abundance of ways that you can save on flights. You just need to identify your scheme and be intentional in your search.

Book Sooner Rather than Later

Numerous people believe that plane ticket prices are less expensive when you wait to purchase them at the last minute, yet researchers decree that the average ticket prices, in fact, tend to increase as the travel date draws closer. There was a time when

---

[55] Ibid.

airlines used to offer huge deals a few weeks out when they were attempting to fill empty seats with leisure travelers, but times have changed. Now, they are able to cover their bottom line, since travelers buy pricey first and business class tickets which means they no longer have to fill every seat on the plane in order to be profitable. Nonetheless, they recognize that business travelers who have unexpected trips arise are still likely to snatch up some of the vacant seats and will pay full price.[56]

According to Expedia's 2019 Travel Pricing Outlook which took into account over fifty billion online flight searches and 295 million flights in 2018, the best time to book flights is three weeks before your trip.[57] Other studies advise that you book fifty to fifty-four days ahead of your desired travel window.[58] In either case, the consensus is that it is better to book your flights sooner rather than later if you want to get a good deal, especially if you have specific dates in mind that you want to travel and/or your dates are during peak travel times like Thanksgiving, Christmas, New Year's Day, or Spring Break.

Utilize Fare Alerts

Practically every major online booking site offers airfare alerts that notify you when there is a decline in fare prices.

---

[56] Bortz and Snider, "Booking Cheap Airfare."
[57] Coyle, "Best Days Book Flight."
[58] Bortz and Snider.

Admired digital resources such as Hitlist, The Flight Deal, and Secret Flying provide fast alerts on good deals. If you sign up for fare alerts from companies like Kayak, CheapOAir, Skyscanner, Google Flights, or Momondo, you can stipulate particular routes and travel dates. Don't discount (pun intended) online travel agencies like Expedia and Priceline, as they sometimes purchase seats from the airlines in bulk and sell them for whatever the market will bear. Consequently, you can benefit from savings if they have overpurchased a specific route and need to sell.[59]

The AirfareSpot.com and The Fare Deal Alert occasionally find mistake fares and post those on their sites. I have alerts set up on my phone through the IFTTT (If This Then That) app linked to the RSS feed for those sites that are triggered for deals associated with my home airport and various travel destinations I am interested in at any given time. This way, I receive a notification as soon as possible before the mistake fares are discovered and addressed.

Scott's Cheap Flights is another popular source for being notified about flight deals. You choose departure airports from which you would like deals and receive email alerts when there are deals associated with those airports. There are free and paid

---

[59] Ibid.

plans available for this service. According to their website, most of the deals are 40 to 90 percent off normal prices.

Be Flexible with Your Itinerary

> *If you are willing to be somewhat flexible with your itinerary, you open yourself up to more opportunities.*

For instance, if your exact flight dates and times are not set in stone from the beginning, you give yourself some wiggle room to make some subtle adjustments that can ultimately save you a significant amount of cash. Some online travel agencies and flight search engines allow you to compare prices with flexible dates covering your preferred dates as well as a few days before and after those dates. Other sites provide color-coded calendars displaying a quick green-yellow-red visual depicting the least expensive, average, and most expensive prices per day. Utilize these features to help you select the best options.

Survey Different Departure Airports

In addition to being disposed to exploring various dates and times, you can also consider different airports of departure. Perhaps, you are within driving distance of two or more major airports. As you are looking for flights, you should see if there are noticeable differences in pricing if you leave from one airport versus another. Of course, you need to factor in how much time and cost are associated with the logistics of your departure airport selection (e.g., driving distance, parking fees, and gas if you drive yourself; shuttle schedules if you take a shuttle, traffic patterns) in order to ensure you're making an accurate comparison.

If you are mapping out a trip where you plan to be gone for several days or longer and you can get a much cheaper flight leaving from an airport hours away, you may consider booking a night at a hotel near the airport that offers free parking and airport shuttle service. This way, you can drive to the city the night before an early morning flight, avoid the stress of same-day travel in unpredictable traffic, and bypass airport parking fees. The money you save from evading the long-term parking cost is more than enough to cover the charge of the hotel stay. Well, what if you're not taking an early morning flight but are instead arriving back from a flight late at night and don't care to drive home that same night? The strategy is applicable in this scenario, also. You can drive to the hotel near the airport, park your car for free, take the shuttle to catch your flight and back to the hotel upon your return from your trip, and spend the night at the hotel. In advance of your trip, you need to make sure that the hotel is on-board with this type of arrangement. Surprisingly, there are some hotels that openly promote this.

Examine Destination Sequencing

If you are taking a trip with multiple travel destinations, look at how the sequencing of your locations impacts pricing. You may be surprised to learn that if you go to City A, then City B, and City C last, you may be charged $150 USD more than if you were to go to City B first, then City C, and City A last. Check it out.

Consider Layovers

Sometimes, having an itinerary with a layover (or two) may be less expensive than booking a nonstop flight. Contrary to popular belief, this is not always the case. So, run the searches, investigate the results, and see for yourself what the numbers look like. Your decision should be based on what is important to you. If you are more concerned about getting to your destination as soon as possible versus saving money, you might not want to even entertain an itinerary with layovers, which is alright. Nonetheless, if you are trying to save money and are open to layovers, you need to set parameters for the quantity and length of layovers you are willing to incorporate into your trip. In other words, you need to determine if a two-hour layover is worth saving $50 USD or if you feel that you would need to be saving more money in order for that length of a layover to be worthwhile. Is there value to having three layovers to save money while dealing with the hustle and bustle of maneuvering through multiple airports and racing to gates to catch your connecting flights? Only you know your tolerance for these types of scenarios.

Maximize Layovers

I would like to take the opportunity to interject that if you are open to layovers and also creative with your planning of layovers, you can actually not only save money but expand your vacation experience. I can share a couple of examples of when I did this.

A few years ago, when I was planning my trip from the U.S. to Rio de Janeiro, Brazil, I realized that because of the location of my departure airport, it was inevitable that my itinerary would include layovers. I noticed there was a wide array of options regarding the locations of the layover airports both domestically and internationally and the layover lengths, ranging from an hour or two to several hours overnight. A few of the layover cities were places I had never been and was interested in exploring, so I decided that I wanted to deliberately have a longer layover at an airport in a city I had never visited in order to add an excursion to my main trip.

I did research on each location to find out how far the airport was from the actual heart of the city and did a brief study of the city culture, seeking something unique and intriguing. Once I narrowed down my list to a couple of places, I conducted a search for companies that provided tours specifically for people interested in participating in city tours during a layover. This way, I knew that they provided transportation from and back to the airport, understood the urgency to return me to the airport on time for my next flight, and had experience sticking to a tight schedule. Recalling all of this, I elected to schedule my layover in Sao Paulo, Brazil. I thought it would be cool to explore more than one city in Brazil to experience a bit of diversity. I looked for a flight itinerary that had the longest layover possible without including an overnight stay (because I personally didn't want to deal with the additional expense and logistics associated with planning that).

With about a six-hour layover in Sao Paulo, I booked a three-hour city tour. The guide gave me an exceptional tour that was focused on the history, culture, art, and food of Sao Paulo and Brazil as a whole. This was an excellent introduction to my time in Brazil and afforded me the chance to discover another city in Brazil that was altogether different from Rio.

My second example of a creative layover experience involves a two-for-one deal I came across some years back. The deal was advertised as a trip to Sydney, Australia, by way of Bali, Indonesia and required that your itinerary include a multiple-day "layover" in Bali. The price of the trip was a little less than it would cost to fly directly from the U.S. to Australia, and I know this for a fact because I had been pricing trips to Australia at the time.

During this period, I knew practically nothing about Bali but recognized that it was a good deal to be able to visit two places for cheaper than it would be to visit one; that's simple mathematics. Long story short, I booked the trip to Sydney with a four-day layover in Bali and absolutely had the time of my life! I had a great place to stay, planned some amazing activities, ate some delicious food, and met some incredible people. Ironically, I actually enjoyed my time in Bali more than in Sydney though Bali was simply my means for cheaper travel to Sydney. To this day, the Bali trip is in my top three.

Needless to say, I am a fan of maximizing layovers. If you have a travel goal to visit as many places as you can, it is an effective way to see more in a shorter span of time for less money. If I had taken separate trips directly to Sao Paulo and Bali, I would have needed more time off from work and funds to cover the transportation and accommodations for the extra trips. So, definitely consider an itinerary with layovers in order to save money on your flights and overall trip from a big-picture standpoint.

Search for Flight Deals

If you prefer to fly exclusively with certain airlines, you may want to start searching for flights on their respective websites. In fact, for some airlines, for example, Southwest Airlines, you are only able to book flights on their website as they do not permit their tickets to be sold or displayed on third-party websites.[60] The main benefit of flying with particular airlines is that if you join their loyalty programs, you can accumulate miles that can be used toward perks like upgraded seats (e.g., from coach to first class), a waived fee for a checked bag, or even free flights.

Some airlines also have branded credit cards that allow you to access even more benefits, as you are able to rack up miles even faster. (So, on a side note, if you are in the market for a credit card and are a frequent flyer [or potential frequent flyer] with a particular airline, check to see if they have a credit card and find out what types of perks they offer.)

A benefit of booking directly with the airline is that it is often the simplest way to book. Also, if a problem arises with your itinerary, you may find it a lot easier to deal with the airline versus a third-party company when trying to get the issue

---

[60] Seemann, "Booking Flights Cheapest Prices."

resolved.[61] Likewise, from personal experience, when I have had issues where delayed flights or flight schedule changes caused me to miss a connecting flight, the airline ticket staff has generally been more accommodating in assisting me with booking another flight when I had originally booked directly through the airline versus a third party.

For budget travel, when searching for flights, I recommend utilizing travel booking engines and online travel agencies (OTAs) because they search multiple airlines at once. Some common sites are those like Expedia, Travelocity, and Priceline. So, instead of searching flights with a specific airline, you can view flights across multiple airlines.

To take it a step further you can utilize metasearch engines or aggregator sites like Skyscanner or Kayak to search several booking engines and OTAs at once. So, a site like Skyscanner will search through OTAs such as Priceline, Expedia, and Travelocity and compile the results from those sites so you don't have to visit those sites individually to search for deals. Aggregators do not supply the capability for you to book on their site, but once you use their site to locate the deal you want, you click to be transferred to the OTA, booking engine, or airfare site

---

[61] Ibid.

where you can book.[62] I recommend that you check a variety of aggregator and booking engine sites because deals may vary across sites, not all airlines are represented on each site, and each site has its own niche, features, and filters.

For instance, Momondo is great when searching for international itineraries as well as last-minute tickets.[63] Relatedly, CheapOAir has a strong performance when it comes to finding good last-minute international fares. However, take notice that CheapOAir's results on flights booked ahead of time are average to sub-par.[64] If you are interested in deals on business class tickets, Momondo and Skyscanner are where you should look. Skyscanner is also known to be an exceptional platform for checking out flights in Europe. Skyscanner and Agoda are recommended sites for searching for flight deals in the United States. In 2020, Skiplagged ranked at or near the top of many lists of best travel search engines for the cheapest plane tickets all around – domestic and international.[65]

If you know in advance that you are planning to book a hotel and/or rental car in addition to a flight for your trip, you can potentially save money by purchasing a package with two or more items together. OTAs and aggregators like Expedia,

---

[62] Bramblett, "Airfare Search Sites."
[63] Holzhauer, "Top Flight Search Engines"; Bramblett.
[64] Bramblett.
[65] Holzhauer; Bramblett.

Travelocity, Priceline, Kayak, Orbitz, Hotwire, Booking.com, and Skyscanner are beneficial for this purpose. Each has its own unique set of features and filters, so visit their websites or apps and get a feel for which ones you like. Not only do you benefit from the savings, but you also enjoy the convenience of having everything booked in the same place.

Kayak has one of the most comprehensive sets of filters, including rare ones such as landing times, layover cities, alliances, in-flight amenities, and aircraft type.[66] Google Flights also has a formidable set of filters to help you ensure that you only receive search results in which you are interested. Some of these include number of stops, layover duration, connecting airports, price ceiling, flight times, airlines and/or airline alliances, and total length of flight.[67]

Priceline, Hotwire, Orbitz, and Travelocity offer opaque booking, which is when select details of the flight such as the departure and arrival times and even the airline are hidden until the booking is complete. Though you can take advantage of some superb deals by utilizing this option, you are not always guaranteed to get the cheapest fares and it does require a bit of flexibility in your schedule.[68]

---

[66] Bramblett.
[67] Keyes, "Google Flights."
[68] Seemann.

Continuing in the vein of flexibility, apps and websites like Hopper, Google Flights, Momondo, and Skyscanner have a visual (usually color-coded green, yellow, and red) fare calendar that shows average prices for days, weeks, and/or months before and after each proposed flight date range. This is helpful if your travel dates are flexible because you can see how shifting your dates can impact the cost of your flights. You can literally save hundreds of dollars based on your date selection.[69]

Now, it's one thing to be flexible when it comes to your departure and arrival dates and times, but what if you are also wide open in terms of your travel destination? If you are not completely locked in to one specific travel destination, you will appreciate Momondo's fun "Anywhere" search and Skyscanner's "Everywhere" option, where you can enter any departure city, and it generates results depicting the cheapest fares from that city.[70] Similarly, Skiplagged offers its "Everywhere" option for the destination, which grants you the ability to search for the cheapest fares available from your desired departure airport.

If you are the type of person who values a good visual display, then you will love the Google Flights map-based search where leaving the "Where To?" field blank lets you see the

---

[69] Ibid.
[70] Bramblett; Seemann.

cheapest place to fly from your desired airport during your selected dates/date range or at any time if you select the flexible dates option.[71]

If your Travel Destination Analyzer results from Step One of this book yielded a large number of locations that fell into Tiers One and Two, you may choose to use tools like the "Anywhere" and "Everywhere" features or map-based search to help you determine your destination according to the prices and dates. Release your nomadic spirit and roam freely.

So, what if you are not quite open to flying anywhere in the world but have a handful of travel destinations you are considering? For example, say that your Travel Destination Analyzer results list Cartagena, Colombia; Nairobi, Kenya; Dublin, Ireland; and Istanbul, Turkey as Tier One options. You can use Google Flights to search for flights from your home city to various destination cities in one search. So, in my example, you could enter the airport code for your home airport in the field for departure city and input "CTG, NBO, DUB, ISL" in the destination city field and review and compare prices to those four destinations. Needless to say, in addition to evaluating flight prices, you also want to reflect on other factors for selecting a

---

[71] Keyes.

travel destination like weather/climate, currency, budget, etc. (see Step One of this book).

If you are planning a trip with multiple travel destinations, you need an aggregator that provides the capability for you to perform a multi-city search. A roundtrip search will only allow you to search for flights from City A to City B, then back to City A, whereas, a multi-city search lets you search for a flight itinerary from City A to City B, from City B to City C, from City C to City D, then back to City A. Nowadays, several search engines offer this functionality, but I have found Kiwi, Google Flights, Momondo, and Skyscanner to be the best for international multi-city searches. I once booked a trip through Kiwi that included six different travel destinations across three different countries, and that is not even including the layovers/connecting flights between some of those destinations. It was a very complex itinerary! Nonetheless, Kiwi made it very simple.

Google Flights doesn't just allow you to do multi-city searches; it lets you do multiple multi-city searches at the same time! You can search up to seven departure cities/airports and seven destination cities/airports in the same query.

Let me give a few examples. So, when I lived in Northern Massachusetts, I would sometimes fly out of Boston Logan Airport and other times fly out of Manchester Airport in New

Hampshire, which was actually closer to me. Say I wanted to take a multi-city trip that included New York City, New York and Chicago, Illinois. With Google Flights, I could search for flights from Boston to New York to Chicago and back to Boston AND from Manchester to New York to Chicago and back to Manchester in the same query, compare the results, and see which yields the cheapest fares. I could break it down even further if I wanted and search for flights from Boston to LaGuardia Airport in New York to O'Hare (ORD) Airport in Chicago back to Boston, from Boston to John F. Kennedy (JFK) Airport in New York to Midway International (MDW) Airport in Chicago back to Boston, AND from Manchester to JFK Airport in New York to ORD in Chicago back to Manchester in the same query and compare the results.

Not to completely blow your mind, but I could also include itineraries where I switch up the order of my destination cities. What if I am open to going to Chicago before I go to New York? I may actually be able to find cheaper fares based on the change in sequence. I have found this to be the case on different trips I have planned and have been able to save hundreds of dollars on each trip by swapping the order of my destinations.

Google Flights is built on the ITA Matrix, which was originally developed for travel agents, and this is why there are a lot of powerful features you can access via Google Flights that are unavailable with other search engines.[72] You can also utilize the ITA Matrix software by Google for free, which supplies you with even more advanced flight searching capabilities. The ITA Matrix is not as user-friendly as Google Flights and can be a bit complicated for novices to navigate, but if you are willing to invest the time and patience to work with it, you can create some complex flight itineraries that can save you money and maximize your trip plan. I typically use Google Flights and/or the ITA Matrix when I am crafting trips with creative layovers because they allow you to dictate which cities you allow for connecting flights and the length of the layover durations. For instance, when I was planning the trip for my two-for-one deal to Australia by way of Bali, I was able to toggle between three to six days of layover in Bali to see how that affected my overall trip cost. That feature is a game changer!

Review Search Results and Be Mindful of These Tips

As you look through the search results on various sites, make sure that you click all the way through each page to the final price so that you are comparing apples to apples. Some sites show you total pricing upfront, while others wait until the very end to add booking fees, taxes, and baggage fees. Sometimes, this information is in the fine print, so you really

---

[72] Seeman.

have to pay attention. There may be times when you may think that you are saving a lot of money only to have those savings be diminished at the end due to steep booking fees. Case in point, Vayama and CheapOAir advertise some good deals upfront, but beware that they are also notorious for their heavy booking fees that range up to $25 USD for domestic flights and $50 USD for international flights with Vayama and up to $100 USD for coach flights with CheapOAir.[73]

Kayak, Agoda, Booking.com, Momondo, and others allow you to view your search results based on the cheapest, quickest, and best overall options. So, whether it is strictly about finding the lowest fare, identifying the most direct itinerary, or having a combination of the two, you can sort the results based on what is important to you in order to make the best decision.

Momondo provides a "flight insight" data feature for your selected city pair, displaying the least and most expensive fares, pegged to season, airline, time of departure, day of the week, and more.[74] Likewise, upon receiving your search results via Google Flights, they offer "flight insights" with tips on how you can save money by making changes like altering your flight dates or departure airport. You then have the choice to decide if you want

---

[73] Ibid.
[74] Bramblett.

to implement the suggestions or proceed with the presented results.

Be aware that in order for some sites to supply you with reduced pricing, they might make subtle changes to your flight itinerary compared to what you entered as your desired trip criteria. For instance, you may input your desired departure date as 07/03 with a desired return date of 07/07, and in your list of results, you may have an itinerary with a return flight on $07/07^{+1}$. That little plus one means that you will actually be returning one day later on 07/08 instead of 07/07. It is a slight difference but can be a major issue if you don't notice it. You may end up missing an event or being late to a meeting on 07/08 because you were thinking you were arriving back home on 07/07.

Another example of a subtle change involves the airport location. You may be searching for a roundtrip ticket, and an itinerary result may have you departing from one airport in the city and returning to a different airport in the city or maybe even a different city altogether. Though it has been over fifteen years ago, I still remember like it was yesterday a trip I booked via Priceline from Chicago, Illinois to Washington, D.C. for an event I was attending. I had someone pick me up from Washington D.C. – Ronald Reagan National Airport (DCA) and return me to DCA airport after the event, only to realize upon arrival that my return flight was leaving from Washington D.C.

– Dulles International Airport (IAD) instead of DCA. Needless to say, with D.C. rush-hour traffic, I had missed my flight by the time we got to IAD. It was a very frustrating ordeal, but it was my fault for not recognizing the subtle difference in the itinerary. Honestly, I was mainly relieved that I did not run into the same type of scenario returning to Chicago given the ORD and MDW airports based in Chicago. Thankfully, I had left from MDW and returned to MDW. I learned my lesson from that situation and have since paid very close attention to the search result details. Please learn from my mistake.

As previously mentioned, Skiplagged ranks among the top for travel search engines. One of the reasons Skiplagged is capable of locating such cheap flights is that it exploits a somewhat controversial savings technique that the airlines aren't so fond of called "skiplagging," which involves a customer buying itineraries that have stops and abandoning some flight legs before the final destination.[75] As opposed to solely searching for tickets from City A to City B, Skiplagged also searches for "hidden-city" tickets – flights from City A to City C that have a layover in City B.[76]

For example, say you want to take a trip to Dallas, Texas. If you search for a flight from Charlotte, North Carolina to Dallas,

---

[75] Ibid.
[76] Holzhauer.

Skiplagged may find an inexpensive flight from Charlotte to San Diego, California that has a layover in Dallas. You could just book that itinerary and get off the plane in Dallas without finishing the entire flight pattern.

Though this practice is rumored to be illegal, it is not. Nonetheless, airlines have been reported to take back airline miles from those who take part in this practice on a regular basis. Not all Skiplagged fares are the result of employing the skiplagging concept. By reviewing the flight itinerary, you will be able to easily identify whether it was or not. If you do choose to take advantage of skiplagged fares, know that you need to be part of #teamcarryon because checked luggage will not be getting off the plane in the city with you.

Many times, when using an aggregator, the lowest fares are found on smaller, lesser-known OTAs rather than the larger ones we have typically heard of like Expedia, Travelocity, etc. If you do come across an OTA you are not familiar with, it does not hurt to do your due diligence to verify the legitimacy, record, and reputation of the company. You can check for reviews online and reference ratings and complaints from organizations like the Better Business Bureau (BBB.org).[77]

---

[77] Bramblett.

Train and Bus Transportation

Riding a train or bus is a viable mode of transportation to your travel destination if you are attempting to avoid a costly flight and are willing to accept the tradeoff of extended travel time. It also affords you the opportunity to savor the scenic route. From an airplane thirty-five thousand feet above the terrain, you are not able to take in the sights of each unique area as you pass through on your way to your destination. Relatedly, when driving yourself as opposed to taking advantage of train or bus transportation, you often miss out on some spectacular views because you are focused on traffic and the road ahead. Enjoying the journey is a simple pleasure not to be taken for granted.

Travel by Train

Amtrak is the sole long-distance, intercity passenger railroad in the continental United States. There are a few intercity passenger railroads that service specific states and regions like Alaska Railroad in Alaska[78] and Brightline Trains which operates in Florida and California (and soon Nevada),[79] but if you are looking to travel by train from the East Coast to the West Coast (or vice versa) or to several cities in between, Amtrak is the way to go. Amtrak has routes in the Northeast,

---

[78] Alaska Railroad, "Route Map."
[79] Brightline, "Homepage."

South, Midwest, and West regions including major cities such as follows:

- Boston, Massachusetts

- New York City, New York

- Philadelphia, Pennsylvania

- Washington, D.C.

- Cleveland, Ohio

- Atlanta, Georgia

- Miami, Florida

- Houston, Texas

- New Orleans, Louisiana

- St. Louis, Missouri

- Chicago, Illinois

- Denver, Colorado

- Phoenix, Arizona

- Las Angeles, California

- Portland, Oregon

- Seattle, Washington

You can also travel from the U.S. to Canada via routes from Seattle to Vancouver and from New York to Montreal and Toronto and vice versa.[80]

Train versus Plane

As of August 2020, via the Amtrak app, if you were to book months in advance, you could purchase a one-way Amtrak coach trip from New York to Los Angeles by way of Chicago for under $200 USD. Keep in mind that the three thousand-mile journey would take three days – one day from New York to Chicago, a brief train transfer, and two days from Chicago to Los Angeles. So, you are looking at a minimum of six days roundtrip. With that said, this would not be the method of travel you would take if you only had a week of vacation available, as you would not really have time to actually spend in L.A. given the lengthy amount of time spent in transit. You would either need to plan to fly or take the trip via train when you had more vacation time available.

If your goal for taking the train is to save money compared to purchasing a plane ticket, then you would be looking to buy coach tickets. The pricing of less than $200 for travel from New York to L.A. is the cost if you were to purchase coach tickets for both legs. You would be in a reclining seat with a decent amount

---

[80] Amtrak, "Amtrak Routes and Destinations."

of legroom for someone of average height and have access to at-seat lighting, a tray table, and an electrical outlet. If you were to upgrade your tickets to the business option, you would gain additional legroom with footrests. The sleeper room options consist of a private room with towels and linens, turndown service, and access to the station lounge and complimentary meals on-board. The main differences between the roomette and bedroom choices for the sleeper room option are that the bedroom has an in-room restroom, sink, and shower and twice the space of a roomette, while the roomette supplies access to a private restroom and shower in your car versus in your room. These upgraded ticket options deliver added comfort and convenience, but they come at a hefty price. For the New York to L.A. trip, the business option has an associated increase of over $100 USD, and the sleeper room option can cost you upwards of over $2,600 USD one way if you were to select the bedroom option for both legs of the trip! If you were to find a good flight deal, you could potentially secure roundtrip coach-plane fare for around the same price as a one-way railroad trip with the business option. Hence, I reiterate that the only way that you could really save money by taking the train instead of a plane is by selecting the coach passenger railroad option.

Train versus Bus

There are a handful of factors to mull over when trying to determine whether to take the train or bus to your travel destination.

In general, bus travel tends to be the cheaper of the two, but train travel is typically more spacious and more comfortable.

Though Amtrak has added free Wi-Fi on most of its routes, express coach lines like BoltBus and Megabus lean towards having even more amenities. Aside from cost, comfort, and perks, routes are a critical component of the selection criteria.

The happy medium for motor coach travel is routes between 125 and three hundred miles, which allows for trips between 2.5 and six hours. Anything longer can seem unbearable in a bus, and shorter trips are recurrently avoided due to many travelers' desire to remain flexible. Moreover, on shorter routes (less than one hundred twenty-five miles), travel times are inclined to be more predictable by train via railroad as opposed to short-hop bus routes on traffic-congested expressways.[81]

---

[81] Schwieterman, "Amtrak's Market Share?"

Also related to routes, the frequency is important. The more often the route is run, the more options you have for the times you can travel. If a route is only run daily, then you are limited to that specific time slot, whereas, if there are three to five trips per day, you have choices. By default, several of the long-distance routes may be offered at a lesser frequency due to the sheer length of the trip. In this case, you will likely travel by train. On the contrary, for short-distance and medium-distance routes, there is severe competition between Amtrak and express coach lines. This is not just involving the likes of BoltBus and Megabus but smaller lines such as Go Buses.[82] With the redundant routes from several sources, your options are plentiful.

Besides route duration and regularity, you must recognize route destinations. Which mode can get you closest to exactly where you what to go? If you are traveling from one major city to another major city, you have an array of opportunities at your fingertips. However, if you are traveling to or from a city that is not as popular, your options are not as abundant. For instance, if you are traveling from St. Louis, Illinois to Chicago, Illinois, there are many buses that run that route. On the other hand, if you are trying to get to Springfield, Illinois, the state capital, there are limited direct routes to that destination. While Megabus

---

[82] Ibid.

runs express between Chicago and St. Louis, only stopping at rest stops along the way, Amtrak's route from Chicago to St. Louis calls on ten intermediate stops, including Springfield.[83] A train ticket may cost more than a bus ticket, but the total trip cost will likely be more expensive if you purchase a bus ticket and then have to pay for a cab, Lyft, or some other mode of transportation to get to your final destination versus utilizing a direct train route.

The last factor for choosing between train or bus is a matter of convenience but also safety. The majority of train traffic is routed through easily accessible and well-populated train stations. You find them in the heart of the city, at airports, and in other prominent locations. Although some cities have dedicated bus terminals connected to train stations, many motor coach pick-up and drop-off points are in relatively remote locations.[84] This may be inconvenient from the standpoint of coordinating travel to and from these locations.

Furthermore, departing from and arriving in unfamiliar territory as a solo traveler can be nerve-racking enough, but if the place seems a bit sketchy, is in a rough-looking area, and/or is not well-lit, your uneasiness and timidity can be intensified. Given this scenario, whether taking a train or bus, it is important

---

[83] Ibid.
[84] Ibid.

to do your research and get a clear understanding of the location and surroundings of your arrival and departure points, especially if you are traveling alone at night.

Additionally, it is important to have a plan in advance in terms of your next steps. You don't want to be arriving near some dark alley in a foreign country after midnight, struggling to connect to Wi-Fi to search for an Uber to get to your hotel only to discover at that time that the country doesn't even have Uber. Some scary situations can be avoided if you plan ahead properly. Even still, persist with vigilance.

Bus Selection

So, say that you have identified bus travel as the best mode of transportation for yourself; now, how do you go about deciding which express coach line to patronize? Well, that will be dependent upon a lot of the aspects I have already discussed for other transportation modes such as cost, route destinations and frequency, pick-up and drop-off locations, and comfort regarding seat and legroom. Some other measures to consider are the reservation and boarding processes, refund and rescheduling policies, deals, amenities, and customer service. I will briefly address each of these.

Whether it is by phone, online, or onsite, most coach companies offer two or more ways to book your travel. If you are paying onsite, you often have to pay in cash. Greyhound Lines is first come, first served, so even if you booked an economy ticket in advance, you might not get to ride if the bus fills before you get a seat. So, you would either need to plan to show up early or purchase a ticket at a higher fare with priority boarding, which guarantees you a seat. BoltBus, a Greyhound entity, provides guaranteed seating with the purchase of any ticket. Similarly, Megabus, owned by Stagecoach Ltd., offers reserved seating. In order to board, some lines require that you present a printed ticket, while others allow you to display an e-ticket on your electronic device.

Practically none of the motor coach lines offer free cancellations or refunds on missed rides when standard tickets were purchased, but some do offer refundable ticket options at a more expensive rate. A few lines will permit you to reschedule for free as long as you do it within a certain number of hours before the original scheduled departure. There are other lines that charge a fee for you to reschedule, no matter how far in advance of your original departure time you do so. Still, there is a small number of companies that don't allow you to reschedule at all. Pay close attention to the fine print as you book your reservations, so you know what the policies are, just in case you need to cancel or reschedule your trip.

Keep an eye out for deals, as some companies extend discounts if you purchase tickets online versus over the phone or onsite, and others such as Megabus advertise promotions that you would see if you follow them on Facebook or Twitter. Trailways presents lower same-day, roundtrip fares to select locations when you travel midweek. Find out if there are other special discounts that you may be eligible for like discounts for students and veterans, which Greyhound offers. Trailways supplies a military discount up to 15 percent to all active-duty members (including their spouses and dependents) of the United States Army, Navy, Air Force, Marine Corps, and Coast Guard. This also encompasses reservists, members of the National Guard, retirees, and visiting foreign personnel. Senior citizen discounts are proposed by some bus lines like Trailways, which allows individuals age sixty-five or older to enjoy up to 10 percent off their regular fare.[85]

The majority of the motor coach lines have rewards programs where with every so many trips you take with them, you receive a free trip. So, if you know that you will be a frequent bus rider, this is a good incentive for you to plan most of your trips through the same company in order to take advantage of the free trips you can accrue.

---

[85] Trailways, "Current Offers & Discounts."

Over recent years, it has become rather standard for motor coach lines to supply free Wi-Fi, and many have power outlets as well. There are those who boast that they show movies on-board or have satellite television for their patrons to watch. This is nice if you are seeking entertainment during a long ride. Supplementary features some customers appreciate are cup holders, free bottled water, reading lights, and small tables.[86]

Customer service is a sticking point for many people. As I read through several blogs and reviews, numerous individuals commented on issues ranging from schedule delays to poor communication to filthy bathrooms and their satisfaction/dissatisfaction for how the problems were addressed. I reiterate that the best way to gain insight on things like this would be to check out customer reviews and business ratings for any of the companies you are considering so that you are able to make an informed decision.

There is an abundance of motor coach options worldwide. Obtain referrals and recommendations, and do your research so that you are able to find the best one for you based on your standards.

---

[86] The Washington Post, "Best Bus Your Buck."

Shuttles

At first glance, it may seem a bit odd to have shuttles listed as a mode of transportation to get to your travel destination. After all, we tend to think about using shuttles to get from place to place around town or to ride to nearby stops. While they are commonly utilized for these purposes (as discussed in the section entitled *How to Get around While There*), they can also be commandeered for short-distance trips.

Taking a shuttle can be considered an alternative to riding a bus or train or driving yourself to a destination. It's typically less expensive than taking a train or renting a car to drive yourself, especially when you factor in gas. While taking a bus is often cheaper than taking a shuttle, depending on the distance, taking a shuttle can be more convenient due to the more frequent routes and availability.

Companies such as Groome Transportation supply park-and-ride shuttle services to major airports from cities that may be an hour or two (or more) away. The primary intent is to provide passengers convenient and reasonably priced transportation and free parking as opposed to their having to drive themselves and pay for expensive long-term airport parking. Nonetheless, this is a good alternative for students traveling to hang out with family or friends for the weekend, those meeting up for a quick girls'/guys' trip, or solo travelers interested in exploring a nearby city. If you're meeting up with people, they can pick you up from the airport. If you're traveling alone, you can, perhaps, catch a free shuttle to your hotel or utilize public transportation or a rideshare service. Ideally, if you are traveling alone, you will book lodging that is centrally located to places you want to visit and activities you want to participate in while in town to minimize the cost of transportation within the city. Otherwise, this scenario of traveling to the city via shuttle might be less convenient and economical versus your driving yourself in your own vehicle because you are able to also use that vehicle for local transportation while at your destination. Calculate the costs and see what makes sense/cents.

A great place to start your search for shuttle services in your area is by visiting www.airportshuttles.com. They are a leader in global travel for airport transfers with service to over two thousand airports. You can also take a look at the websites for SuperShuttle Express and GO Airport Shuttle Service. Lastly, you can do an internet search for airport shuttle services in your local area.

Rental Cars

By far, the biggest benefit of driving a rental car to your travel destination is that it affords you a considerable amount of flexibility. You are not constrained by departure and arrival times correlated with cruise or flight itineraries or train, bus, or shuttle schedules. You can pretty much come and go as you please. Also, you have that same level of convenience while you are at your vacation spot because you are able to use the rental for your local transportation as well. You are not having to rely on or pay for additional transportation. Of course, you will need to factor in associated costs like gas and parking fees into your budget to account for these expenses.

Speaking of parking, you will need to plan ahead to ensure the place where you want to lodge has onsite or nearby parking available. You also want to get a feel for what parking is like around town in terms of availability and ease of accessibility. You can accomplish this by making inquiries in your Facebook travel groups, investigating on the internet, or speaking with people at the location as you seek out information about specific activities to participate in, venues to visit, and a place to stay.

For relatively long distances, driving a rental car versus your own personal vehicle is an affirmative alternative because it allows you to minimize the amount of miles and overall wear and tear you put on your personal vehicle. For shorter trips, five hours or less roundtrip, it may not be as cost-effective to rent a car versus drive your own vehicle if your vehicle is in fairly good condition. Crunch the numbers and decide accordingly.

There are a few drawbacks to driving yourself to your travel destination. Obviously, you don't have the luxury of casually gazing out the window at the captivating sights, reading a book, checking out your phone or tablet, or taking a peaceful nap while someone else is driving. Instead, you have to be focused on the road, making sure you're going the correct way, and possibly navigating through traffic, construction, inclement weather, and anything else along your path. None of these things are really deal breakers though if you don't mind driving.

Renting a Car for Travel within the United States

The process for renting a vehicle in the U.S. for travel within the U.S. is fairly straightforward. Typically, you must be at least twenty-one years old and have held a driver's license for a minimum of one year. A handful of agencies such as Avis will rent to eighteen-year-old drivers; however, Hertz has a minimum age requirement of twenty-five years old. Several rental car agencies tack on a daily surcharge for drivers under the age of twenty-five.[87]

You need to have adequate liability insurance. If you have standard car insurance, this is often suitable coverage, but you need to check your policy details to verify. If you pay for the rental car with a credit card, your credit card company may

---

[87] Just Landed, "Car Rental the US."

supply a free collision damage waiver (CDW). Find out the specifics from your card company. If you do decide to purchase the third-party insurance that may be offered through the rental car agency, know what it does and doesn't cover. Some policies only cover you for in-state travel, and there may be a weighty surcharge for travel between states if that is even an option. In certain areas, some agencies restrict travel to in-state or within a particular region. For this reason, it is important for you to gain a solid understanding of the parameters of the rental agreement when you are shopping around for a rental car.[88]

Rental cars are categorized by class or body size (e.g., economy, compact, mid-size or intermediate, full-size or standard, premium or luxury, convertible, sports car, or SUV), and these categories impact the price you pay. Other factors contributing to cost include the day of the week and the season during which you rent, the size of the town, and the popularity of the local tourist attractions. For tips on how to acquire deals on rentals, refer to the end of this section concerning rental cars.[89]

---

[88] Ibid.
[89] Ibid.

Driving a Rental from the United States to Canada or Mexico

In general, if you are driving to a country outside your native land, you need to acquaint yourself with signage, symbols, lights, language, rules, and regulations common to the area. If you are seeking to drive a rental car across the border, particularly from the United States to Canada or Mexico, there are some things you need to know. Bear in mind that the following information pertains to processes and procedures for vehicles rented in the United States. Practices may differ when renting in Canada or Mexico.

From the USA to Canada

Many rental car agencies will allow most rental vehicles to be driven from the U.S. into Canada; however, there may be restrictions regarding specific vehicle classes. For example, Enterprise, Alamo, and National car rental agencies prohibit vehicle classes like exotics, large passenger or cargo vans, or specialty vehicles from traveling outside of the United States.[90]

It is wise to make the rental agency aware of your travel plans in advance so that the right accommodations can be made. Before traveling, you should also familiarize yourself with your

---

[90] Enterprise Rent-A-Car, "Rental Mexico and Canada"; Alamo, "Rental Canada or Mexico"; National Car Rental, "Rental Canada or Mexico?"

personal insurance coverage, so you know exactly what you have. This way, when you get to the counter at the rental car agency and they put forward various options, you have a better idea of what you need and what you don't. You will definitely need a non-resident insurance card, which is also known as a yellow card. This card validates that you have auto insurance for travel in Canada. If you are in an accident in Canada and do not have a yellow card, you can be liable for a fine. Companies like Avis and Budget supply you with a card free of charge when they have been informed in advance of your plans to drive the rental into Canada.[91] Be prepared to present your passport and driver's license. In fact, it is helpful to have a couple of copies of each handy so that you have them just in case they are needed during your trip.

Limited locations of some rental agencies near the U.S./Canada border will consent to one-way rentals depending on the availability at the location.[92] So, if you desire to drive to Canada but take a different method back to the States, a one-way rental is an option to consider. Travel rules vary by company and location, so be sure to thoroughly read the terms and conditions before booking your reservation.

---

[91] Avis Rent a Car, "Avis Rental Mexico Canada"; Budget Car Rental, "Canada Cross-Border Car Rental."
[92] Ibid.

From the USA to Mexico

No car rental agencies appear to offer one-way rentals to Mexico.[93] Strictly speaking, if you pick up the rental in the States, you need to return it in the States. For Alamo, National, and Enterprise, most locations do not even permit roundtrip travel from the U.S. to Mexico.[94] Hertz, Dollar, and Thrifty have select locations that can manage reservations from the United States to Mexico with a scheduled return to the United States. These locations are in states that border Mexico – California, Arizona, New Mexico, and Texas. As a renter, you are required to purchase Mexican insurance at the counter in one of these states from the respective Dollar, Thrifty, or Hertz brand. "Mexican border patrol requires that a renter be covered under a Mexican insurance policy in order to enter Mexico, as the policy provides the renter/occupants and vehicle with legal compliance upon crossing the border."[95] The policy includes the following coverage:[96]

- Liability for injury and/or damages to third parties

- Collision and comprehensive coverage for the rental vehicle

---

[93] Michael, "Rental Car into Mexico?"
[94] Alamo; National Car Rental; Enterprise Rent-A-Car.
[95] Hertz, "Mexico Travel Insurance."
[96] Hertz.

- Theft of rental vehicle

- Medical expenses for vehicle occupants

It should be stated that if you do not purchase the insurance and are in an accident, you may be subject to arrest, and your rental will be seized.[97]

Plan to present your passport and license to the rental agent, for they will be necessary to make the reservation and process the insurance policy.[98]

In addition to the insurance policy, if you are a non-Mexican resident seeking to drive from another country across the border into Mexico beyond the free or border zone, you will need a Temporary Vehicle Import Permit (TIP) as well. The free or border zone is the area between twelve and sixteen miles (twenty to twenty-six km) from the USA-Mexico border. For instance, cities like Tijuana, Mexicali, Nogales, and Ciudad Juarez are within the zone and do not require possession of a TIP to visit, but driving to Mexico City, which is outside the zone, would require that you have a TIP. You can obtain a TIP through Mexico's national bank, Banjercito.[99]

---

[97] Michael.
[98] Hertz.
[99] Ibid.

Budget and Avis, likewise, have select locations that allow travel into Mexico, but they have a few more stipulations than Thrifty, Hertz, and Dollar. In addition to being a U.S. resident, informing the agents at the rental counter of your plans to travel into Mexico, and purchasing the insurance from them, they also specify that you have a corporate account with them and if you are not a U.S. citizen, you must have permanent residency in the U.S. or a valid visa. If at least one of these requirements is not fulfilled, you are not eligible to rent a car from Avis or Budget to drive into Mexico.[100]

In summary, be sure to do your research before your trip to find out which rental car agency and exact location you will choose, and meticulously review the terms and conditions for the reservation.

Locating Deals on Rental Cars

There are many different tactics you can employ when searching for the best deals on rental cars. A lot of it boils down to your personal preferences and priorities as well as your method for planning other elements of your trip.

---

[100] Avis; Budget Car Rental, "Mexico Cross-Border Car Rental."

Low-end Rental Companies

If you are looking for cheap prices and are not into all of the bells and whistles that top-end loyalty programs have to offer, you may want to check out the low-end rental agencies like Alamo, Payless, and Thrifty. They are not guaranteed to always have the lowest prices but can be a worthwhile place to start.[101]

Agencies with Loyalty Programs

On the contrary, if you are an active participant in loyalty programs, you may want to search for deals on the website of your favorite car rental agencies. Some agencies even partner with airline loyalty programs and allow you to earn airline miles in lieu of car rental agency points (though there may be recovery fees associated). These agencies do not pledge to propose the least expensive prices at all times either, but with the loyalty programs, the accumulation of miles and/or points results in long-term savings that can be beneficial over time.[102]

Special Discounts

Some rental car agencies extend discounts to senior citizens. Sometimes, the agencies advertise this, and sometimes they don't. So, be sure to ask, just in case. You don't want to miss out on any deals if you are eligible. Certain organizations grant

---

[101] Perkins, "Best Rental Booking Sites."
[102] Seemann, "Finding Cheap Car Rentals."

discounts on rental cars to their members. For instance, AAA members have access to discounts on rentals from particular agencies. If you have a Costco membership, you can also save on car rentals.[103] AARP has a partnership with the Avis Group where they promote discounts of up to 30 percent for car rentals through Avis, Budget, and Payless.[104] It's hard to beat that deal! Research to find out the details of the various discounts, and if you are eligible, don't forget to reference your affiliation at the time of booking.

Metasearch Engines and Online Travel Agencies

My personal strategy is to start my search with metasearch engines and online travel agencies (OTAs). Even if you lean towards low-end rental companies or agencies with loyalty programs, it is insightful to check the metasearch engines and OTAs to gauge whether or not you are getting a good deal. Some examples include Expedia, CarRentals.com, and Rentcars.com. I usually begin with Kayak or Hotwire because I have used them for several years for planning multiple aspects of my trips, I have their apps on my phone, and I am familiar with the layout of their site and features. They help me identify which agencies have the lowest prices. Then, I often visit the websites of those agencies to see if I can get an even better deal, especially if I

---

[103] Sheehy, "Cheapest Way Rent Car."
[104] Perkins.

participate in their loyalty program, as neither Kayak nor Hotwire have a loyalty program. If I get the better deal by booking directly with the agency, I will often go ahead and reserve the car with the agency.

Opaque Booking Rates

If I plan on renting the car for a while (i.e., four or more days), I may return to the Kayak and Hotwire sites to check out their opaque booking rates. For Kayak, they are called Surprise Agency rates, and for Hotwire they are called Hotwire Hot Rate deals. Similarly, Priceline has Express Deals, and Momondo has Surprise Agency bookings.[105] These opaque rates are typically the cheapest; however, as previously inferred, you do not find out the name of the rental agency until after you complete your transaction. This can be a bit of a risk, plus these fares are normally nonrefundable.

Things to Look out for When Booking a Rental Car

As you look through the various websites for rental car deals, it is important to take certain precautions, and regardless of the company you choose to go with, you must review the terms and conditions before finalizing your purchase. Here are some common occurrences to which you need to pay attention.

---

[105] Seemann.

- As you are going from website to website to compare prices, ensure that you are clicking all the way through to the end to reveal the total pricing that includes taxes and/or fees. A lot of sites reel you in by advertising base pricing to make it seem that their prices are lower than their competitors, when in actuality, they are not.[106] Their competitors are displaying the total pricing upfront. So, make sure you are comparing apples to apples.

- Many sites advertise big savings with "Pay Now" deals. The downside of these deals (which is not always clearly communicated) is that they are usually nonrefundable.[107] This is not a bad thing if your plans are definite, but if you have not quite solidified everything, then you might need to hold off on buying anything that cannot be refunded if your plans change.

- Likewise, be aware of the cancellation policy. A lot of deals with great prices have hefty cancellation penalties attached.[108]

- Rental car agencies at airport locations are inclined to be more costly due to higher per day fees and airport

---

[106] Ibid.
[107] Ibid.
[108] Perkins.

concessions fees and taxes. Given this information, you might want to think about renting from an off-site location. Be sure to factor in and compare any expenses you may incur to travel to one agency location versus another.[109]

- Most deals include unlimited mileage, but occasionally, there will be a deal that has a mileage cap.[110] Be on the lookout for this, just in case.

- Notice the differences between size and cost of the cars as you are comparing rates. Sometimes, the cheapest deals are for "mini" or "economy" cars that are not practical for medium- to long-distance travel, and the price for the car the next size up is only a couple more dollars a day. So, it would be well-worth the upgrade.[111]

Personal Vehicle

Driving your personal vehicle to your travel destination is probably an underrated yet viable option, especially for shorter distances. You reap all the benefits that you would if you were to rent a vehicle, with the added bonus of not having to pay a daily or weekly rental rate. Plus, you get to drive something that you

---

[109] Seeman.
[110] Perkins.
[111] Ibid.

are familiar with and comfortable with versus having to try to figure out the odds and ends of a borrowed ride. Not to mention, you don't have to worry about coordinating the pick-up and drop-off scheme. Even better, you can bypass all the website research and planning that you would have to endure with any of the other transportation options discussed.

Nevertheless, there are a few legitimate reasons why you may not want to drive your own car. As aforementioned, a downside of driving your car versus a rental car is that you are putting miles and general wear and tear on your car as opposed to the rental car. Another scenario may be that your personal car is unreliable, and in which case, you would feel safer and more secure driving a rental car that is dependable. Lastly, perhaps, you just don't like your car and would prefer to drive something newer and/or better-looking than your car. Well, that's okay, too. If you can afford to splurge, then why not do so?

This concludes the section on *How to Get There*, which focused on modes of transportation to get you to your travel destination. This next section is geared toward providing information about transportation options you can utilize once you have arrived at your travel destination.

How to Get around While There

Shuttles

Shuttles can be a very convenient and cost-effective method for getting around town. Most often, they have predestined routes to specific locations like to and from the airport, hotels, and event venues. Because of these frequent, recurring routes, prices are often relatively reasonable and on occasion, even free.

Many hotels and resorts offer complimentary transportation from the airport to their facilities and vice versa, especially if they are located within close proximity from one another. Likewise, hotels that are located in a downtown area or near popular tourist attractions may provide free shuttle rides to well-known sites. These are certainly things to inquire about in Step Four as you are selecting where you will be staying during your trip.

In addition to investigating your place of lodging for shuttle access, you should also look into shuttle services to common event venues such as theme parks or convention centers if these are places you plan on frequenting while in town.

Subways/Trains

Train Travel in the City

When it comes to intercity train travel, you've got your above-ground rail systems and your underground systems that I am categorizing as subway/metro trains. Much of the material I share in this section is applicable to trains in general, but I am focusing on subway/metro trains.

Subway trains are an economical and convenient mode of transportation for getting around in large cities. Riding the metro is a wonderful way to experience the town as the locals do. Furthermore, in metropolitan areas with gridlocked traffic, you can reach your destination in town a lot quicker via subway versus bus, taxi, or rideshare.

Subway Basics

If you've never ridden the metro before, from the outside looking in, it can appear to be a somewhat overwhelming and/or intimidating experience. However, once you get the hang of how they operate, it's actually relatively simple. Here are a few basic tips that can be applied to practically any metro system in the world and will have you riding like a pro in no time!

1. First, familiarize yourself with the proper name of the subway system as well as the name the residents in the

area call the system. Knowing the nickname will help get you in the local mindset and cut back on possible confusion upon arrival because you and the locals will be conversing in the same language, so to speak. For instance, in England, the London Underground metro system is affectionately known as the Tube, and in Norway, the Oslo Tunnelbane rapid transit system is commonly called the T-banen or T-bane for short.[112] You can discover the proper and slang names by doing an internet search for the city plus the words *metro, subway,* or *train system.*

2. Once you know the system name, get a hold of a map so that you can study the naming scheme for the lines and stations that make up the system. The lines represent the different paths within the system, and the stations are the various stops on the line where you can get on or get off the train. The lines may be identified by a proper name, letter, number, and/or alphanumeric combination and are often color-coded. The colors are extremely beneficial because they allow you to easily trace the path of the metro line on the map, and they serve as another way to reference the line. For example, people frequently denote the line color as the line name such as the Red

---

[112] Sam at EF, "Riding Metro in Europe."

Line or the Blue Line. You can access a city's metro system map by looking it up on the internet or by downloading an app on your phone or tablet. My preference is to download an app on my phone because I can view the map before my trip as well as during the trip in real-time at the metro station and on the train. Plus, the apps generally offer a lot more information and features than just the map.

3. After becoming acquainted with the map, you can begin locating stations that will be important to you during your trip. Upon completing Steps Three and Four of this book, you will know what you plan on doing and where you will be staying while on your trip, and if you plan to utilize the metro as your main source of transportation for your trip, you should find the metro stations closest to your activities and place of lodging. Determine the best routes. Notice that there will often be more than one route you can take to get from Point A to Point B. Look for the most direct and cheapest routes. The fewer the transfers, the better. In other words, if you can walk a block over to get to a station that allows you to hop on a train on the Green Line which will take you to a stop leading directly to your desired destination, do that as opposed to getting on a train on the Orange Line,

transferring to a train on the Purple Line, and then switching to a train on the Yellow Line to get to your desired destination. Keep it simple.

4. Before heading to the subway to go somewhere, you should know:[113]

   A. The name of the station where you will be getting on the train.

   B. The line you will be taking.

   C. The name of the last stop on the line you will be taking.

   D. The name of the stop where you will be getting off.

   E. The name of the stop immediately before the stop where you will be getting off.

   F. Any connections you need to make in order to transfer to other lines (if applicable).

   You obviously want to know what line to take and your points of entry and exit on the route (i.e., A, B, D, and F), so you know how you will get to your destination.

---

[113] Jo, "Metro Trains in Europe."

Additionally, you must know the name of the last stop on the line you will be taking (i.e., C) to ensure you are taking the train that is traveling in the direction you want to go. Just because you make it to the correct station and get on the correct line does not mean you're headed to your desired destination. For simplicity's sake, let's say you recognize that you need to take the Fruit Line that only has four stations on it – Apple, Banana, Cherry, and Dragon Fruit. Your desired destination is near Cherry Station. You arrive at Banana Station, which is between Apple and Cherry on the route. There may be a track where there are trains heading towards Apple and a separate track where there are trains heading towards Cherry or a track that may have trains going in either direction at designated times. At the station, there will be signs indicating trains going toward Apple and trains going toward Dragon Fruit. You want to get on a train on the Fruit Line heading toward Dragon Fruit because when you get on that train, the very next stop will be Cherry Station. (Side comment: I must smile because by using this food analogy, I have managed to make myself hungry.)

The signs displaying direction may be on or near route maps at the station, at the train platform where you are to board the train, and/or on the trains themselves. Many stations have a digital sign above the stop showing a short description of the train line or destination station along with the anticipated arrival time. Some stations also audibly communicate this type of information as well as any delays or last-minute changes over an intercom system, so listen up for the announcements. Be sure to double-check the train line and direction before you get on the train.

Once you are on the train, look for a visual map of the train line indicating the stops on the route. Many trains have a system with lights that represent where your train is as it approaches each stop. The names of the stops are generally uttered over the public announcement system as well. It is ideal to be aware of the stop right before the stop where you are to get off (i.e., E), so you are prepared to exit once you reach your stop. On most trains, the doors are open for merely seconds at each stop, and if you are not near the door when it opens, you may miss your opportunity to get off, especially during rush hour when the subway is crowded and there are several people aggressively trying to get on and off at the same time. In situations like this, a good practice is to start gathering yourself and safely making your way closer to the door BEFORE you reach your stop.

5. Be mindful that some cities have more than one metro system. Sometimes, there will be a main metro system that handles transportation in and around the city center and supplementary systems that have train lines that branch out from the city into the suburbs or other neighborhoods/areas on the outskirts of the city boundary. Each system has its own set of lines and stations, and you can make a distinction between them according to their system name and logo. Per your destination, you can travel between systems as needed, but observe that you may not be able to use the same tickets or cards between systems. To avoid confusion, you may want to study up a little on the metro systems as you are planning your trip if you think you will be traveling the city by train.

Tickets, Cards, and Passes

Purchasing Tickets

The subway ticketing process varies from city to city and occasionally, from station to station within the same city. There are stations that utilize paper tickets, plastic cards, or a combination of the two. Tickets and cards may be representative of a ticket for a single trip, multiple trips within a designated timeframe, or a particular dollar-amount's worth of trips. Paper tickets are almost exclusively available for purchase onsite at a metro station. In some larger stations like central stations, you can frequently stand in line to purchase tickets from a person at a ticket counter where you can pay via local currency, debit card, or credit card. Nevertheless, in most main stations you operate ticket booths or machines to purchase tickets electronically. Some may only accept cash (i.e., coins or small-denomination bills), while others may merely take debit or credit cards. Learn in advance what is customary for the city you will be visiting, so you will be prepared with the correct form of payment upon arrival at the station.

Buying and Refilling Cards

In many cities, the plastic cards are preferred if you know that you will be riding the train for multiple days because the cards are reusable and reloadable. This means that you can purchase one card to use over and over again as you add more money to the card. The cards are commonly for sale at airports, local retailers, and train stations. You can usually add money to the cards at these locations via local currency, debit card, or credit card; the acceptable method of payment varies per location. In some countries, you even have the convenience of adding more money to the card online or through an app. Sydney, Australia's Opal card supplies this flexibility.[114] More often than not, however, you will use machines at the metro station to refill your card with funds.

Using and Validating Tickets

Some metro systems require you to insert your ticket or card to pass through the electronic barrier as you enter the station, in which case, you would retrieve the ticket/card on the side of the barrier. For other systems, it is sufficient for you to tap/touch/scan a card reader with your ticket or card to enter the station. Keep your ticket or card with you after you enter the station, as there are stations where you have to scan your ticket or card as you board the train, exit the train, connect at other lines, or exit the station.

In some European metros, when you purchase a paper ticket from a ticketing machine, it is not ready to actually use until it

---

[114] McLaughlin, "Getting Around Sydney."

has been validated. Validation is accomplished by your inserting the ticket into a ticket validating machine that time stamps the ticket to signify the start of your trip validity. This way the duration of ticket validity can be tracked according to the type of ticket you purchased (e.g., ninety minutes, twenty-four hours, five days).[115] It is unwise to attempt to game the system by not validating your ticket. Sure, you may get away with a few free rides, but is it really worth the risk? There are ticket inspectors who randomly check passengers' tickets for validation, and if you are caught fare dodging, you will either be faced with paying a heavy fine (e.g., a few hundred dollars in some nations) or spending time in a local jail.[116] I'm urging you - just validate the ticket.

Deciding on Trip-based Tickets or Time-based Tickets/Passes

In some cities, in addition to having the option of purchasing a trip-based ticket (also known as a point-to-point ticket), you can buy a time-based ticket or pass. With a trip-based train ticket, you are paying for your ride from Point A to Point B, whereas, with a time-based ticket or pass you are paying for unlimited trips that occur within a designated period of time (e.g., twenty-four hours, three days). If you are only going to be taking a couple of train rides throughout your trip, it

---

[115] Kwan, "Beginner's Guide Metro Systems."
[116] Kwan; Go-today, "Navigating Metro Stations."

makes sense to buy trip-based tickets, as it would be the cheaper option. However, if you are going to be relying on trains as your sole or primary method of transportation each day on multiple days throughout your trip, it may be more cost-effective to purchase a pass. Not to mention, some cities allow you to use your pass not just for trains but for payment on other modes of transportation, too.

To give you a frame of reference, let's use Shanghai, China as an example. On Shanghai Metro, trips under six kilometers are priced at ¥3. To travel from downtown Shanghai to Hongqiao Railway Station or Hongqiao Airport would cost you ¥7. To go from downtown to Pudong Airport would cost you ¥9. You can purchase a one-day pass for ¥18 for twenty-four hours of unlimited rides or a three-day pass for ¥45. The pass would be in the form of a Shanghai Public Transportation Card that is refillable and can be used on Shanghai trains, metros, buses, taxis, and ferries and on public transportation in neighboring city Suzhou. The card costs a refundable ¥20 and can be purchased at the ticket desk in any station.[117] If you are planning to spend three days in Shanghai, taking a train to and from the airport, to various tourist attractions, out to eat, and out on the town for entertainment, you can very well save a substantial amount of

---

[117] Context Travel, "Practical Facts Shanghai's Metro."

money by purchasing a three-day pass versus several trip-based tickets.

Train Travel out of the City

So, say your trip itinerary includes multiple destinations. Perhaps, you flew from the U.S. to Madrid, Spain, and after spending a few days in Madrid, you plan on heading to Barcelona, Spain and then Paris, France and so on because you intend on spending an entire month traveling throughout Europe. For trips like this, it may be beneficial for you to travel by train. Here is some information about various train options on different continents.

Africa

When you have the option to travel Africa by train, it is overwhelmingly the recommended choice, especially in contrast to travel by road because train transportation is customarily safer and more comfortable. Pricewise, second-class train fares are comparable to or even cheaper than bus fare. Sleeping compartments and first- or second-class carriages are more costly yet still a minimal price by Western standards and, on occasion, allow you to travel in style. Per Lonely Planet, "some high-class train carriages are like little wood-paneled museums of colonialism." A drawback is that aside from trains in Southern and Northern Africa, trains tend to be very slow, and long delays are typical. Trains primarily operate in West Africa and South Africa with restricted services in other parts of the continent, and cross-border operations are scarce.[118]

Here are some of Africa's quintessential train journeys:[119]

- Nairobi–Mombasa (Kenya)

- Zouérat–Nouâdhibou (Mauritania)

- Dakar–Bamako (Senegal and Mali)

- Transgabonais (Gabon)

- Windhoek–Swakopmund (Namibia)

- Pretoria–Swakopmund (South Africa and Namibia)

Asia

Traveling Asia by train is a fabulous way to enjoy views of the city, suburbs, and countryside. You can experience the luxury of a vantage point not afforded to those traveling by road. Be aware, however, that the trains in Southeast Asia frequently run late and typically have extended journey times.

Beyond that, Thailand, Malaysia, and Vietnam have excellent rail networks. In Thailand, there are popular daytime and overnight train routes going from Chiang Mai to Bangkok,

---

[118] Lonely Planet, "Africa/Practical Information."
[119] Ibid.

Bangkok to Nong Khai (to cross the Laos border), and Bangkok to Surat Thani. If you choose to take a sleeper train, you will have a private bed with curtain. There is either an air conditioner or fan and meals, snacks, and tea are available for purchase. By train, you can travel from Kuala Lumpur, Malaysia to Bangkok in approximately twenty-six hours. The International Express takes you from Bangkok through the entire length of Peninsular Malaysia to Singapore. In Vietnam, trains connect the northern capital city of Hanoi (as well as Sapa, Halong Bay, and the Chinese borders) with Ho Chi Minh, the largest city in the South. The complete journey takes thirty-four hours with no stops. The train is a fun and cheap method of travel in Vietnam, plus sleeper trains can be significantly more comfortable and safer than night buses in areas where there are winding roads.[120]

Numerous options for train travel also exist in China within and between major cities. Unlike the trains in Southeast Asia, the trains in China are generally punctual. So, if you are looking to go out of town, make sure you show up to the station early to allow enough time to stand in long lines outside the main station entrance and to get your luggage scanned. The two main categories for long-distance trains in China are regular trains and high-speed trains, with the latter being faster and more luxurious but also more expensive. K, T, and Z class regular trains travel at

---

[120] South East Asia Backpacker, "Book Transport Southeast Asia."

top speeds of 120, 140, and 160 km/h, respectively. High-speed D class trains can reach up to 250 km/h, while C and G class high-speed trains can achieve up to 350 km/h.[121]

A few years ago, I took an overnight, D class sleeper train from Shanghai to Beijing, departing at about 7:00 PM and arriving around 7:00 AM the following day. The ticket was less than $100 USD. The bed was comfortable enough for me to get some well-needed rest after having spent my final day in Shanghai trekking through the city, trying to capture my last few highlights. The space was a bit tight, so if you're even mildly claustrophobic, you may want to avoid a sleeper train unless you upgrade your ticket for a more spacious arrangement. There wasn't much to see at night during the journey in the dark, but the two crucial benefits were that I was able to save money on accommodations for the night and I got to travel to my next destination while I slept. I woke up the next morning rejuvenated and ready to embark upon a fresh set of adventures in a new city!

Travel via railway is limited in Laos, Indonesia, and Cambodia, but you may be interested in the routes that are available. In Laos, a three-kilometer stretch of rail links Nong Khai (Thai border) with Vientiane (the Laos capital). The eight-

---

[121] Lonely Planet, "China/Getting Around/Train."

hour train ride from Jakarta to Yogyakarta is a popular course for those traveling in Indonesia. If you are looking to access Cambodia by rail, you can visit Phnom Penh, Takeo, Kampot, and Sihanoukville.[122]

Australia

Taking the scenic route through Australia via train is an expedient and inexpensive way to travel the continent. NSW TrainLink supplies services between Sydney and the regional centers of New South Wales including the Blue Mountains, the Central Coast, Newcastle, Wollongong and along Australia's east coast to Melbourne, Brisbane, and Canberra. V-Line trains connect Melbourne with regional hubs in Victoria, and TransWA traverses Western Australia.[123] Queensland Rail operates the high-speed *Spirit of Queensland* service between Brisbane and Cairns.[124]

There are noteworthy rail journeys such as the *Ghan* and *Indian Pacific* run by Great Southern Rail that traverse across Australia, exhibiting comfort and a sense of sentimental romance. The *Indian Pacific* meanders between Sydney and Perth with stops at Broken Hill, Adelaide, and Kalgoorlie. The legendary *Ghan* travels between Adelaide and Darwin, taking in

---

[122] South East Asia Backpacker.
[123] Tourism Australia, "Travel around Australia."
[124] Lonely Planet, "Australia/Practical Information."

Australia's Red Centre and the tropical Top End. Also operated by Great Southern Rail are the *Overland* which runs between Melbourne and Adelaide and *Great Southern* roving between Brisbane and Adelaide.[125]

Europe

For travelers who reside outside of Europe, you are eligible to buy a Eurail pass that allows unlimited train travel for specified periods of time either in an individual country of your choosing with a Eurail single-country pass or across thirty-plus European countries with a Eurail global pass. Eurail passes let you travel on all the regularly scheduled trains run by the participating national train operators, including high-speed, intercity, overnight sleeper, regional, and suburban. Additionally, Eurail passes cover a variety of smaller private train operators and in several cases, local and regional trains where you can simply jump on and present your pass as you are requested. Recognize that you are required to pay a minimal fee for a seat reservation on many long-distance and high-speed trains and for sleeping berths on overnight trains. You can do this at the station as you go or beforehand sometimes online or solely by phone.[126]

---

[125] Tourism Australia.
[126] The Man in Seat 61, "Use a Eurail Pass."

There are two types of Eurail passes: continuous passes and flexi passes. Continuous passes permit unlimited travel every day for a continuous period of time – either fifteen days, twenty-two days or one, two, or three months, starting on any date you select. These offer supreme freedom and flexibility, but in order for you to get your money's worth, you need to be traveling by train every day or two.[127]

Flexi passes are more economical if you plan on staying put for some days between each train ride. Flexi passes are offered in increments of four, five, seven, ten, or fifteen days of unlimited travel within an overall one- or two-month period. Say, for example, you purchase the five days in one month pass. The overall one month commences on the date you validate your pass at a station. You can use each of your five days of unlimited travel any time during that one-month timeframe, on whatever dates you prefer, just by writing the date in one of the five boxes printed on your pass each time you want to use one of your travel days. All one-country passes are this flexi type.[128]

While a Eurail pass is affordable and convenient because of the flexibility it affords you if you plan on visiting numerous cities within a European country or various countries within Europe, it is not always necessarily the cheapest option. In fact,

---

[127] Ibid.
[128] Ibid.

point-to-point train travel in Europe is frequently cheaper than purchasing a Eurail pass *if* you have specific travel dates *and* you book your reservations months in advance. With a Eurail pass, you can pretty much determine where and when you're traveling somewhere on the fly as long as there is availability on the train. This is an advantage, but it does come at a premium. Whether you choose to purchase a Eurail pass or point-to-point tickets is basically dependent upon your budget, the quantity of destinations you intend on visiting in a given period of time, and how structured/solidified your travel plans are.[129] For more details about the Eurail pass, go to the official website, www.eurail.com.

South America

The presence of trains has gradually diminished throughout South America; nevertheless, there are still some fantastic routes that remain available. Uruguay is in the process of investing in the revitalization of its old lines. Similarly, Ecuador has spent a substantial sum of money in the rehabilitation of its old lines. In fact, the Nariz de Diablo (Devil's Nose), an exhilarating, steep descent through narrow switchbacks between Riobamba and Sibambe, has become one of many of the popular tourist routes in Ecuador. Here are some other remarkable routes throughout

---

[129] Ibid.

South America that allow you to take in the beautiful scenery while experiencing a hint of old-fashioned railroad train nostalgia:

- Curitiba – Paranaguá (Brazil)

- Oruro – Uyuni – Tupiza – Villazón (Bolivia)

- Santa Cruz – Quijarro and Yacuiba (Bolivia)

- El Alto – Tiwanaku (Bolivia)

- Lima – Huancayo – Huancavelica (Peru)

- Puno – Juliaca – Cuzco (Peru)

Buses

Earlier in Step Two, in the *How to Get There* section involving bus transportation, I discussed the advantages and disadvantages of travel via bus as well as bus selection criteria from the perspective of bus travel in North America, mainly the United States. While many of the foundational principles apply to domestic and international bus transport alike, there are some crucial differences according to the region of the world. Here, I provide some specific details regarding bus travel in a variety of locations.

Information by Destination

Africa

In Africa, public bus prices typically range between $3 USD to $30 USD, depending on your total travel distance. These buses are primarily used for travel within the city or between major city hubs where a good network of sealed roads exists. In general, they tend to be comfortable, safe, and spacious.[130] In rural areas, where there are few or no sealed roads, the buses are ancient and very overcrowded with people, livestock, and goods.[131] They make repeated stops for passengers and bus breakdowns.[132]

International bus services are relatively prevalent throughout the continent. In the wealthier African states, you may get a choice between the luxury air-conditioned coaches with reclining seats, extra legroom, on-board toilet, movies, and complimentary coffee and tea and the alternative rough old European reject minibuses with nonfunctioning air conditioner, questionable engineering, no toilet on-board, and some people standing because there are more passengers than there are

---

[130] Nomadic Matt, "How to Travel Africa."
[131] Lonely Planet, "Africa/Practical Information."
[132] Nomadic Matt.

seats.[133] However, in some regions, the minibuses are your only option.

African minibuses don't operate on a set schedule; departure is based upon capacity. They do not leave until absolutely every seat is occupied.[134] For this reason, it is impossible to predict exactly when you will leave. It may take minutes for a minibus to fill, or it may even take hours. So, if you plan to travel by minibus, it is essential for you to have a very flexible itinerary. Nonetheless, bear in mind that this characteristic is not necessarily a negative thing. During periods when the minibuses are filling quickly, they make more frequent trips. If you were to travel by coach which has a set timetable, you may end up having to wait until the next day for the next scheduled bus, while you may be able to catch an earlier trip the same day via minibus given the multiple trips they take per day. In addition, minibuses make random pickups along their route. If they are heading in the direction you want to travel, you can just flag them down and they will let you embark. This flexibility is convenient for the person getting on the bus, but for those who are on-board what may already be a packed, hot bus, adding more people exacerbates the level of discomfort, while also extending the overall length of the trip.

---

[133] Lonely Planet.

[134] Where the Road Forks, "The Ultimate Guide to Bus Travel in Africa."

Although, minibuses may make many stops within and near towns, during long-distance stints, there may be long stretches of the trip when there are no stops. They are known to travel six or more hours straight. Given that there is no toilet on-board, it can be an awkward and uncomfortable situation if you drink a lot during the trip. With that said, you truly want to regulate your liquid intake if you are riding a minibus. If you have an emergency where you absolutely have to relieve yourself, worst-case scenario, you should be prepared to beg or bribe (with a few dollars in local currency) the bus driver to stop along the side of the road for you to handle your business. Moving on…

Minibuses will pretty much take you anywhere you want to go, including the farthest villages and outposts. Coaches normally travel exclusively between major cities. If a coach route encompasses your travel destination, you benefit from taking the coach over a minibus because the limited stops and defined timetable equate to a shorter and faster trip.

The biggest advantage to taking a minibus over a luxury coach is the cost. Currently, minibus prices range from $0.50 USD to $1 USD per hour of travel, whereas, you can expect to pay approximately $1 USD to $2 USD per hour of travel for a coach ticket.[135] Half off is a gigantic savings and totally worth it,

---

[135] Ibid.

particularly if you are on a tight budget. The coach tickets are still extremely cheap, though, when you compare them to the cost of plane or train tickets, and if you crave structure, consistency, comfort, and reliability, the value of purchasing a luxury coach ticket over a minibus ticket might outweigh the cost.

In terms of safety, I must mention that auto accidents in Africa are not uncommon largely due to the fast driving speeds there. Here are a few tips to help optimize your safety when traveling by bus.[136]

- Select the safest seats available on the bus. Theoretically, these are aisle seats towards the middle of the bus opposite of oncoming traffic.

- Try to travel in the newest, safest buses that you can. The newer buses are equipped with safety features that the older buses do not possess.

- **When you have the option to travel by coach as opposed to minibus, it is recommended that you take the coach.** Professionals operate the coaches, and their reputation matters to them. So, they have an incentive to strive to ensure that you and your personal items arrive at your destination safe and sound.

---

[136] Ibid.

Asia

Most towns in Asia have buses for local transport. There is also a broad variety of buses utilized for long-haul journeys. They travel virtually everywhere, especially in Southeast Asia, departing at just about any time, day or night. They range from the notorious "chicken buses" in Indonesia where you're literally sharing a ride filled with people, goods, and chickens, to the luxurious, air-conditioned VIP buses in Thailand with reclining seats, movies, and snacks. In any case, you are in for quite an adventure!

In essence, there are two categories of buses: those that the locals primarily ride and those that tourists primarily ride. The ones tourists take hit up all the popular routes like from Bangkok to Surat Thani to visit the Thai islands of Koh Samui and Koh Phangan.[137] These types of destinations are mainly frequented by "out-of-towners" as opposed to residents. The tourist bus routes are more direct and have fewer stops than the local buses that continually stop along the way as people hail rides. As a result, the tourist buses maintain a more consistent schedule, whereas, the local buses' actual timetable shifts widely based on the number of stops.[138]

---

[137] South East Asia Backpacker.
[138] Rodgers, "Buses in Asia."

The local buses can end up getting fairly crowded, especially since drivers seldom consider the bus to be "full." Drivers allow passengers aboard as long as they can pay, regardless of if there are vacant seats or not. Also, you pay the same fare whether you are able to grab a seat or have to stand, as the fare is based on the distance traveled.[139]

Many of the standard long-haul tourist buses are air-conditioned, have toilets, and even show movies. Some tourist buses are deemed VIP buses, which means that they generally have the features of a standard tourist bus as well as some potential added amenities such as snacks and/or Wi-Fi.[140] Many of the overnight VIP buses in Thailand and Malaysia have reclining seats and some of the ones in Vietnam tilt back, becoming actual beds. Rarely are any of these features or amenities available with local bus services. Tourist buses can also be safer than local buses because drivers are required to abide by certain regulations that they are more likely to adhere to when tourists are involved, as they would rather not have to deal with a scandal that could damage their reputation and bottom line.[141]

---

[139] Ibid.
[140] Ibid.
[141] South East Asia Backpacker.

So, you may be wondering, "What are some of the advantages of taking a local bus?" Well, I'm glad you asked. The biggest perk is the cost. Local buses are much cheaper than tourist buses, but neither are expensive. In Thailand, a local bus from Bangkok to Chiang Mai may cost you 100 Thai Baht (about $3.33 USD), while a VIP tourist bus may cost you 800 Thai Baht (about $26.66 USD);[142] a standard tourist bus fare would fall between those two prices. (Side comment: When you are given the chance to choose between a regular tourist bus fare and a VIP bus fare, make sure you inquire about the differences. Some companies will run a scam where they charge you to "upgrade" from a regular ticket to a VIP ticket, which means you are physically on the same standard bus as the regular ticket-paying people, but your upgraded VIP status connotes that your ride comes with sugary snacks, which is inequivalent to the difference in price.)[143]

Another benefit of taking a local bus is the flexibility. Maybe, you're the nomadic type who likes to go with the flow and not be tied down to a set schedule. Then, local buses may be right up your alley.

Third, local buses travel to several places not covered by tourist bus routes. If you want to ride a bus to venture out to

---

[142] Ibid.
[143] Rodgers.

some of the more remote areas or even to locations that are less like cheesy tourist attractions, you will need to take a local bus. Last but certainly not least, something you gain by taking a local bus is the authentic experience of riding with the locals. Striking up interesting conversations and creating lasting memories...There's simply nothing else like it.

Here are a few helpful tips regarding bus travel in Asia:

- Booking – The process for booking bus tickets varies from location to location, but to be on the safe side, for long-haul travel, it is best to book a minimum of a day before your trip, in person at the station. Alternatively, you can typically book through a travel office or at a reception desk, but it would cost you more due to the commission tacked onto the price. Either way, be sure to hold on to your ticket and receipt, as you are unlikely to be reimbursed should you lose your ticket but may be able to get a replacement by presenting a receipt.[144]

- Hailing – If you choose not to purchase a ticket in advance, you can hail a bus heading in the direction you would like to travel by raising your hand and pointing it to the ground in front of you with your palm turned downward. Going this route, you will get a ride but not

---

[144] Ibid.

necessarily a seat. Upon boarding the bus, ensure that you ask the driver the final destination so that you verify you're, in fact, on a bus going to or toward where you desire to go.[145]

- Paying – On several buses in Asia, you do not pay as soon as you step onto the bus. Many times, once the bus has begun the ride, an assistant will come by to collect your money. Your fare will be based on the distance of your trip. It is a good practice for you to have a variety of denominations of bills/coins so you can pay the exact amount because the assistant may not have much change available.[146]

- Selecting a Seat – If you purchase a ticket beforehand, you may or may not have an assigned seat. If you are, indeed, able to choose your own seat, be selective. If the roads are unpaved and/or rough, the most stable seats are generally going to be the ones in the middle of the bus. Try to stay away from sitting in seats located directly on the front or rear axles because you will feel each and every bump, but if you have no option, place a blanket or jacket underneath yourself to help absorb some of the impact. The seats positioned in the front of

---

[145] Ibid.
[146] Ibid.

the bus, those in the center in the back of the bus, and the ones facing the access stairs are considered less safe. Seat belts are seldom supplied. Sit in a seat that has another seat directly in front of it, as this will limit your travel distance in the unfortunate event of an accident. Resist the temptation to choose the seats that have more legroom. Often, these "no-survival seats" are left vacant by locals because they know that they are not as safe.[147] Trust me – safety trumps comfort every time.

- Air Conditioning – Buses without air conditioning can be uncomfortably hot and stuffy, especially when the blazing sun is beaming into the bus and the passengers inside are packed like sardines. However, sometimes, air-conditioned buses can equally become a nuisance when they're cranking out freezing cold air. Make sure you have a jacket handy just in case you need to combat the extremely cold temperatures. Also, refrain from sitting beneath the air conditioner, as sometimes, condensation can drip from the unit and you do not want to deal with a wet mess, particularly on a long trip. Now, that would truly be annoying!

---

[147] Ibid.

- Using the Facilities – Most long-haul buses have the squat-type toilets on-board. These can be a challenge to utilize when the bus is dipping and swaying down the road. Usually, when the bus stops for breaks, the public restrooms will have at least one stall with the type of toilet we're accustomed to using in the United States. So, at the stop, be prepared to get off the bus and walk quickly to the restroom to beat the long lines. The breaks are often short, so you need to handle your business with efficiency.[148]

- Crossing Borders – Buses are usually the most hassle-free mode for crossing land borders in Asia. At times, direct buses connect towns on either side of the border, with a well-organized stop for border formalities. When this is not the case, you simply take a bus to the border, proceed through departure and immigration formalities, and then get on another bus on the other side of the border to continue your journey.[149]

- Knowing when to Exit – Whether you are riding a local or long-haul bus, make sure you let the driver or assistant know your intended destination if you do not plan on riding the bus all the way to the final

---

[148] Ibid.
[149] Lonely Planet, "Southeast Asia/Practical Information."

destination. Preferably, you want to do this shortly after getting on the bus, especially for local transit so that they may help alert you when the bus is approaching your stop.[150]

Australia

There are affordable and reliable bus networks in all major cities across Australia. In Sydney, bus fares spread from around $2.24 AUD (about $1.69 USD) for under three kilometers of travel to $4.80 AUD (about $3.62 USD) for eight kilometers or more. As is the case in several cities, Sydney's buses are largely utilized at night and to connect between train stations. They are also principally advantageous in coastal neighborhoods, such as the Northern Beaches and the Eastern Suburbs, and outer suburbs that don't have rail connections. Given that there are hundreds of overlapping routes across the city, buses are frequently the fastest mode for reaching your destination. Often, you will need to hold your hand out to hail a bus or else the driver will probably pass you by as he/she proceeds along the route.[151]

On the whole, coaches traveling long distances are furnished with comfortable adjustable seating, air conditioning, reading

---

[150] Rodgers.
[151] Ibid.

lights, and a decent toilet.[152] Some also have free Wi-Fi and USB ports for charging electronic devices. All coaches are declared non-smoking.

Australia's national coach company Greyhound operates in every state except South Australia and Western Australia. They offer hop-on, hop-off short trip passes and flexible passes for popular routes based on the distance you seek to travel. In addition, they supply discounts for seniors, students, and children. Regionally, Firefly Express runs between Sydney, Canberra, Melbourne and Adelaide. Integrity Coach Lines is the chief operator in Western Australia, while V/Line supports Victoria with a mixed network of buses and trains. Premier Motor Service covers the east coast from Eden to Cairns and extends flexible hop-on, hop-off fares.[153]

Canada

In general, buses in Canada tend to be clean, comfortable, and dependable. They are non-smoking. Potential amenities consist of on-board toilets, air conditioning, reclining seats, complimentary Wi-Fi, and movie viewings. For long trips, the buses stop every few hours for meals, normally at highway service stations.

---

[152] The Aussie Specialist Program, "Coach Travel."
[153] Lonely Planet, "Australia/Practical Information."

Nationwide, Greyhound Canada has drastically reduced its bus service. The remaining routes largely connect in the east and to Vancouver. For coverage in other areas, travelers must rely on regional carriers for transport.[154]

For service in various parts of Québec such as Montréal and Québec City, check out Autobus Maheux, Intercar, Limocar, and Orléans Express. If you are seeking to travel between Montréal and Toronto, you should consider going with Megabus or Coach Canada, which will cost you about $70 USD. Also, Coach Canada, Ontario Northland, and Parkbus supply transportation between Toronto and other parts of Ontario. Ebus links Vancouver, Kamloops, and Kelowna, while Skylynx runs numerous daily buses between Vancouver and Whistler. Tofino Bus joins all core population centers on Vancouver Island and also offers connections (via ferry) to Vancouver. Maritime Bus serves New Brunswick, Prince Edward Island, and Nova Scotia. In order to hit up the key cities in Alberta, ride with Red Arrow. Going to Newfoundland? You can utilize DRL Coachlines.[155]

For Greyhound Canada, you can purchase your tickets at the bus terminal or online, but for some companies like Megabus, you can only make reservations and buy your tickets online.

---

[154] Lonely Planet, "Canada/Practical Information."
[155] Ibid.

Often, you get cheaper rates online, and tickets are typically less expensive the earlier you purchase them.[156]

Central America

Bus travel is extremely common in the nations that make up Central America. Local buses are regularly available and very inexpensive. In fact, they can be as cheap as one to three USD. They are usually not all that comfortable because they are typically packed, since they are rarely considered full. These "chicken buses" are similar to those I described as being used in Asia; they transport not only people but many sorts of goods and animals like goats and, yes, chickens. The buses in Central America, however, are usually old, retired U.S. yellow school buses that have been driven down through Mexico.[157] They are easily identified by the bright colors with which they have been painted. The ride may not always be the smoothest and there may be the occasional mechanical breakdown along the way, but rest assured, you will get to your destination alright. Minibuses exist to provide connections from hub cities to smaller towns via short-haul trips. These are known as *colectivos* in Mexico and Costa Rica, *rapidos* in Honduras, and *chivas* in Panama. They are a low-priced alternative to riding a first-class long-distance bus, so I suggest that you take advantage of them when they are

---

[156] Ibid.
[157] Steph, "Bus Travel Central America."

173

available. Nonetheless, I must mention that a downside to riding them is that they make frequent stops, so the trip duration can be rather lengthy, and they can get a bit crowded compared to long-distance travel buses.

First-class and some second-class long-distance buses leave the bus station at predesignated times. Others depart from parking-lot bus terminals once the bus is full; there is no set schedule. Departure frequencies also fluctuate. Recall that a number of cities have multiple bus stations and some bus companies may have their own bus terminals. Do your research ahead of time, so you are familiar with exactly where to go.

Beware of the potential danger associated with taking long-distance night buses in the region, as they have become popular targets for highway robbers. This does not apply to those running in Mexico and Panama though. I actually had a positive night bus experience riding from Cancún, Mexico to Belize City, Belize. The trip was $54 USD on an ADO (Autobuses de Oriente) bus. ADO, pronounced "ah-day-oh," is one of the biggest bus companies in the world and Mexico's leader in the bus industry. The coach was spacious and comfortable and had power outlets, Wi-Fi, and a bathroom. The air conditioner was blasting cold air; I'm glad I had a jacket to wear to keep me warm and cozy as I slept. We left the bus station in Mexico around 11:00 PM and arrived in Belize around 9:00 AM the next morning. There were a handful of stops along the way to pick up and drop off passengers at different cities on the route. We also stopped at the border entering Belize, disembarked the bus, and presented our passports to officials. Upon returning to our same bus, we rode a few miles and made a second stop where we got off the bus and entered a building to go through immigration. After that, we got back on the bus and traveled into the city to the main bus station.

If you are planning a multi-country trip, you need to know what the entry/exit requirements are before you travel to ensure you have the appropriate documents and currency (as needed for fees) and can anticipate what to expect regarding the overall border crossing process. Take notice that it is often mandatory for you to change buses at crossings, and you might end up having to walk a few hundred yards across the border or catch a *colectivo* to a nearby bus station.[158] You may be required to pay a land departure fee when leaving Belize to either Mexico or Guatemala (20 U.S. dollars or 40 Belize dollars).[159] In order to cross the border from Costa Rica to either Panama or Nicaragua, you need to pay an exit tax fee of $8 USD at a branch of Banco de Costa Rica (BCR) or another designated payment collection point BEFORE arriving at the border station to avoid possible

---

[158] Lonely Planet, "Central America/Practical Information."
[159] Fodor's Travel, "Taxes."

last-minute difficulties crossing.[160] Theoretically, there is a border agreement between Guatemala, Honduras, El Salvador, and Nicaragua, permitting travel for up to ninety days in the four-nation region, so you shouldn't have to pay to cross into those countries. However, in practice, there are typically some "fees" required at any border.[161]

Europe

In Europe, buses are commonly used for taking short trips around the city or accessing remote villages. Many times, buses are the sole option for reaching mountainous regions. People can utilize services at the small train stations to get them to a point where they can then transfer to a bus that can transport them to their final destination which is inaccessible by train.[162] Buses are typically a tad cheaper than riding a train but are also slightly slower. Bus reservations are seldom needed. On several city buses, you customarily purchase your ticket from a kiosk or machine just before your trip and validate it upon getting onboard the bus.

For the most part, international buses for long-distance travel tend to be less expensive than trains, but the trade-offs are that they are also less comfortable, aren't as fast, and have less

---

[160] U.S. Embassy in Costa Rica, "Payment of Exit Tax."
[161] Lonely Planet.
[162] Steves, "Europe's Long-Distance Buses."

extensive schedules. Some exceptions, however, are Croatia, the Czech Republic, Greece, large parts of Ireland, Morocco, Portugal, Spain, and Turkey, where trains are generally the better (or only) choice. Even nations with substantial rail networks may have certain connections where the bus is more direct and/or quicker than the train.[163]

In the majority of European nations, bus routes are run by multiple companies, each having its own timetables and rates. FlixBus is the leading bus company in all of Europe.[164] Among deals, they offer an InterFlix Pass for €99 (about $120 USD) that covers up to five trips in three months nearly anywhere in Europe via their network of buses.[165] Eurolines, Europe's largest organization of international buses, is composed of many national companies.[166] On their site, not only can you book a specific trip, but you can also look into deals that permit you to travel expansively across dozens of cities throughout Europe over multiple days. To peruse the most comprehensive inventory of European bus companies for the best routes and fares, check out the travel search website Omio.[167] Omio also has an app

---

[163] Ibid.
[164] The Backpacking Site, "Travel Europe by Bus."
[165] Steves.
[166] Lonely Planet, "Europe/Getting Around/Bus."
[167] The Backpacking Site.

where you can book your reservation and access mobile tickets.[168]

Middle East

Within the majority of Middle Eastern cities and towns including those situated in Oman, Qatar, and the United Arab Emirates, there is either a minibus or bus service offered at considerably inexpensive rates. These services tend to be speedy with consistent routes that sometimes have designated stops. Nevertheless, it can be very challenging for visitors to determine exact bus routes and stops because they are rarely displayed and when they are visible, they are more than likely depicted in the local language. If possible, see if you can solicit the assistance of a resident who speaks your language to help you figure out the best way to get to your desired destination by bus.[169] My suggestion is that you first inquire with the staff or host at your place of lodging for basic instructions and then confirm that information once you arrive at your departure location. If this is not an option for you, what you can do is, within a safe space for pedestrians (preferably at a bus stop if you can find one), stand alongside a major road that connects other roads in multiple directions on the side aiming in the direction you seek to

---

[168] Ibid.
[169] Lonely Planet, "Middle East/Practical Information."

travel.[170] As buses slow down when approaching you, speak aloud into the driver's window the local name or landmark nearby where you want to go.[171] Based on the driver's response, you should be able to verify whether or not the bus will take you where you seek to go. You need to be somewhat familiar with what your destination and/or area surrounding it looks like so that you can recognize when you must exit the bus.

For travel between Middle Eastern cities and countries, buses are a common, and often, the only mode of transportation. The good thing is that they are typically dependable, though the fares and level of comfort range from one end of the spectrum to the other. Passengers seldom adhere to the non-smoking policy and the videos shown on-board are usually played awfully loud,[172] so it is doubtful that you will get to nap unless you are an exceptionally hard sleeper.

South America

In major cities and towns, local buses can cheaply get you to famous sites around town as well as some of the more rural areas. In Buenos Aires, Argentina, riding the *colectivo* is a great

---

[170] Ibid.
[171] Ibid.
[172] Ibid.

way for you to visit the neighborhoods of Palermo, Recoleta, or Puerto Madero, which are popular among tourists and expats.[173]

The Transmilenio, a series of rapid transit buses in Bogotá, Colombia, spreads widely through the city. Most of these buses have designated lanes, which is great because they do not have to compete with the hectic and, at times, frustrating mainstream traffic. The Septima line is an exception, as it runs in common traffic with other vehicles, but it is worth taking if you're seeking to journey to Usaquen, one of Bogotá's prettiest neighborhoods.[174]

The Recife Metro subway/light rail system in Brazil includes over fifteen stations that have bus terminals onsite. The immense bus network administered by at least eighteen different companies operates about 4,800 buses that disseminate among the city. Furthermore, Recife has a bus rapid transit system comprised of two road corridors in the city with forty stations, servicing approximately 116 passengers daily. Both bus systems not only get you around town but also supply the means for you to travel to bus terminals in the outskirts offering routes to other cities within Brazil.[175]

---

[173] Jennings, "Around Buenos Aires Safely."
[174] Ryan, "Transportation Systems South America."
[175] Recife metro map, Brazil, "Metro of Recife."

Generally speaking, with regard to long-distance travel, the bus transport systems across South America are rather developed. Though, it must be noted the proficiency and civility of the drivers and condition of the roads and buses can fluctuate greatly from one place to another. When it comes to road conditions, it's largely dependent upon the environment during particular seasons. For instance, massive deserts of red dust in the dry season transform into oceans of mud during the rainy season. Overall, roads tend to be better in Argentina, Uruguay, Ecuador, coastal and southern Brazil, and the majority of Venezuela. Some of the best-maintained roads and most comfortable and reliable bus services on the continent exist in Chile and much of Argentina.[176]

Just about every major town or city has a bus terminal, or *terminal de autobuses* or *terminal de omnibus*. The name differs by nation. In Brazil, it is called a *rodoviária*. In Ecuador, the locals refer to it as a *terminal terrestre*. Many times, they are located just outside of town, requiring you to catch a cab or city bus in order to get to them. The larger, nicer ones offer amenities such as restaurants, shops, and showers and often have cheap lodging options available nearby. The so-called village "terminals" in the rural areas are not the formal depots you may

---

[176] Lonely Planet, "South America/Transport/Bus."

be accustomed to, as they are actually more like dirt lots where ancient buses pass through with someone yelling out destinations.[177] Do your research ahead of time, so you have a basic idea of what to expect prior to your arrival.

Security Tips for Bus and Train Travel (and Crowded Areas in General)

Because using public transportation is such a popular and convenient way to get around major cities, bus/metro/train stations can be very crowded, especially during peak hours of the day. Unfortunately, sometimes, there are thieves who take advantage of the situation by robbing tourists and others who may not be as aware of the potential threat. There is no need to be excessively fearful of utilizing public transportation. You just need to take a few precautions as you should already be doing in any crowded and/or unfamiliar area. Here are a few tips to assist you with this.

1. When carrying a wallet or mobile phone, do not have it in your back pocket, as it would be easy for someone to casually bump or slide up against you to pick your pocket without you even realizing or suspecting anything. Instead, keep these items in your front pockets or, better yet, inside a compartment of your bag or

---

[177] Ibid.

clothing that can be zipped up or sealed in some other manner.

2. If you are carrying a purse or laptop bag, ensure that it is closed and properly fastened. You should have one that has a strap that can be draped over your shoulder and worn across your body. This is a safer alternative to carrying these items by handle(s) in your hand, making you more vulnerable for a snatch-and-grab scenario where someone could simply run off with your stuff.

3. To the backpackers, do not wear your backpack on your back! People can come behind you and take things out of the pockets unbeknownst to you or pull the bag off and run in the opposite direction from which you are facing. Rather, wear the backpack in front, where it is fully visible to you and more challenging to steal.

4. When riding the bus for long-distance travel and you have multiple bags, do not store anything of value in the bags that are stowed underneath, on top of, or in the back of the bus out of your sight. At a minimum, keep your valuables in a bag you retain with you at your seat, away from the aisle area. Better yet, preserve your possessions on your person, preferably concealed.

5. For long-distance bus trips, when you do have luggage stored in places accessible from the outside, try to secure a seat on the bus on the same side as your luggage so you can keep an eye out from your window as people disembark before you in the event that someone attempts to grab your luggage.[178]

Safety Tips for Bus and Train Travel

Aside from tending to the security of your belongings, you should also take action to maintain your personal safety. Reflect on the following advice.

1. Mind the gap. This is a phrase I have heard over public announcement systems in subways throughout the world. It means that you need to watch your step as you are getting on or off a train because there is a gap between the subway platform and the train. You do not want to accidentally step in that gap onto the track, as it can be deadly. Also, note that you may need to step up or down slightly when entering/exiting the train.

2. As you get on a train or bus, make sure you move yourself, your clothing, and belongings away from the doors before they shut. In most cases, whatever does not

---

[178] Rodgers, "Buses in Asia."

clear the doors before they close will be trapped until the doors open at the next stop. You know why this is an important tip, so I will spare you the gruesome details of the possible consequences.

3. Many buses and trains take off immediately after the doors shut, so quickly take a seat or grab hold of something to help steady yourself. You don't want to stumble into something or somebody or fall. Avoid hurting your body and your ego.

4. In some major cities on busy streets, buses don't pull right up to the curb, even when there is a line of people waiting.[179] At times, buses might barely come to a complete stop to let people on and off, so you need to be ready and prepared to move when the bus gets to your stop, so you don't miss your entry or exit. Also, watch your step.

5. When boarding or exiting a bus, especially in a high-traffic area, be sure to look out for speeding motorists around the bus as well as cyclists in the bike lane.[180] You don't want to be caught off guard and involved in a collision.

---

[179] Jennings.
[180] Ibid.

Aggregators, Apps, Maps, and Timetables

There are several resources at your fingertips for making your life easier when researching and preparing to travel by train or bus. For starters, I recommend that you utilize an aggregator to explore your transportation options. Websites like rome2rio.com, omio.com, and 12go.asia allow you to search and compare routes and fares for train and bus rides as well as flights. This is good because you may initially think that you want to take a train or bus ride because you're trying to save money but discover from one of these sites that you can actually get a flight for roughly the same price and arrive to your destination sooner and more comfortably. Rome2rio covers pretty much all continents except Antarctica and is available via an app in addition to the website. Omio includes searches for Europe and North America, while 12Go focuses exclusively on Asia and Australia. In addition to choosing between plane, train, or bus, you can select between a variety of companies for each mode of transportation to compare fares and routes. You can book tickets through these sites months in advance of your anticipated trip.

In many nations, the Google Maps app, one of my major "go-to" apps, is useful to check out train and bus routes in real time or hours or days ahead of time. The beauty about using the app in real time is that you can track your progress on the route and see upcoming stops and transfers. This feature really came in handy when I traveled by bus in Washington, D.C. and Los Angeles, California.

Note that you cannot purchase tickets through the app. Also, be aware that Google services like Google Maps are not available in some countries such as China. In China, specifically, you can utilize maps via Baidu, a Google competitor that could be considered its equivalent. Otherwise, whether in China or another country that does not permit the usage of Google services, you can utilize a virtual private network (VPN). Per Adam Marshall of TechRadar, a VPN is "a piece of software that helps to make you more anonymous online, encrypts your internet use, and lets you effectively trick your laptop or mobile device into thinking it's in another location."[181]

TechRadar presents a list of what it deems the best fifteen VPN services in 2021. Ranking among the top of their list are ExpressVPN, NordVPN, and Surfshark. Each of these services offers a free thirty-day trial period, which gives you a chance to try them out before selecting one of their various paid plan options.[182]

There are also free VPN services available via apps on your smartphone. Check the app store, read the reviews, and do your

---

[181] Marshall, "Best VPN Service 2021."
[182] Ibid.

research prior to downloading. I personally utilize a free app because I so infrequently need a VPN that it is not justifiable for me to pay a monthly or annual fee. Nevertheless, there are some paid services available that advertise relatively reasonable rates. If you are concerned about the security or functionality of using a free VPN, a "best-of-both-worlds" option would be for you to just use a free trial period of a paid service during the time of your trip. This works well if you don't plan to be in the location longer than a month and you rarely travel to destinations where you feel a VPN is necessary. Whether you decide to go with a paid or free service, I recommend that you install the VPN prior to your trip because you may be blocked from doing so abroad in nations where there are restrictions.

With over fifteen million downloads, Moovit is another popular app for searching transportation options across the globe. While you are not able to book tickets through the app, you are capable of receiving route suggestions and directions for transportation by bus, light rail, subway, ferry, car, bicycle, and foot based on real-time data. Moovit provides step-by-step instructions detailing how to get to the station and guiding you all the way through to your final destination. You receive notifications on arrival times and alerts pertaining to delays and service changes. Maps of stations, routes, and lines are accessible offline.[183]

If you want to travel by train in the U.S., the Amtrak app is a critical resource that allows you to search schedules, book tickets, and track the routes in real time. If you favor websites over apps, you can attain the same functions by going to www.amtrak.com. An app with more extensive North American coverage is WanderU, which is great for locating train and bus deals in the U.S. and Canada. It covers eight thousand destinations spanning twenty nations, but selections are limited in Mexico and Europe. A beneficial feature of the app is that it supplies basic information about amenities such as snacks, power outlet and Wi-Fi availability, air conditioning, and restrooms. WanderU also offers a loyalty program incentivizing repeated bookings.[184]

Deutsche Bahn possesses the most comprehensive online timetable for European train travel. Their website is www.bahn.de/en, and there, you can search by city, station, stop, or address. The app version of this website is called DB Navigator. It's free, but it does require a Wi-Fi or mobile data connection. Railplanner, on the other hand, is a free train timetable app that you can download onto your smartphone to

---

[183] Fried, "Best Train Apps."
[184] Ibid.

view train times and calling points without being connected to Wi-Fi or mobile data. It's extremely fast and includes nearly all the trains covered by the DB Navigator app. With it, the entire European timetable resides on your smartphone, with automatic updates downloaded every month. It's geared toward Eurail and Interrail passholders but can be helpful to any user.[185] In order to search for both train and bus tickets in thirty-six European countries, you can utilize the Trainline app (or website at thetrainline.com). Through the app, you can indicate seat preferences, compare fares, and collect points and discount benefits. There are multiple payment options available to purchase your e-tickets, including PayPal and international credit cards.[186]

Other advantageous apps are the public transportation apps that are specific to a certain country or city. You can find these types of apps by searching for them in the Apple App Store or Google Play Store, using keywords like the country or city name plus *metro, subway, transit, map,* and/or the name of the city's metro or transit system. Take a look at the sample screens for the app and read the reviews to vet the app. Additionally, pay attention to whether or not the app can be accessed while offline, as this is preferred just in case you won't have Wi-Fi or a stable

---

[185] The Man in Seat 61, "Train Travel in Europe."
[186] Fried.

internet connection. Once you download the app, while you are connected to the internet/Wi-Fi, it's a great idea to take screenshots of timetables, schedules, and precise routes that you plan on taking so you can quickly access them whenever you need them, even when offline. I found this to be really helpful when I was traveling via the metro in Beijing, using the Metro China Subway app.

If you are the type who likes to have a hard copy on hand, you can always print out maps and directions to carry with you or purchase a guidebook before your trip or soon after you arrive at your destination. You can also buy a timetable book at the train station or travel office. Generally, metro timetables stay the same for a whole calendar year, so you can actually print out a copy of a timetable and be set for your trip.[187]

Taxis and Rideshares

If public transportation options are not available at your travel destination or you prefer not to utilize them for whatever reason, you may choose to catch a ride via taxicab or rideshare. You may also find riding in a taxi or rideshare vehicle viable alternatives if the places you will be frequenting within your destination are relatively close to one another. This section

---

[187] Go-today, "Navigating Metro Stations."

focuses on disclosing the pros and cons of using taxis/cabs and rideshares such as widespread apps like Uber, Lyft, and Grab.

Taxis are the tried-and-true method of the two choices, as they have been around for quite some time now, and virtually everyone is familiar with them. The concept of ridesharing is comparatively new, springing up in the early 2000s. For those of you who are not as accustomed to the concept, essentially, a rideshare is a platform that allows riders to book trips through an app and have the funds deducted directly from a designated account. Using the app, riders enter their basic contact and billing information and desired destination, and from there, can choose from a variety of vehicle options ranging from the driver's own ordinary car, to an SUV, all the way up to a luxury or premium vehicle, if available. The length of existence of taxis versus rideshares does not imply that one is better than the other because of age; each actually has its place depending on the circumstance. Here are some topics to mull over as you decide whether to go with a rideshare or a taxi.

Taxis versus Rideshares

Availability and Accessibility

Availability and accessibility are huge factors in determining which service to choose. Both taxis and rideshares tend to be pretty prevalent in several major cities throughout the world. Rideshares are also available in many suburban areas, and some rural locations, while taxis tend to only be available in some suburban and rural areas. In busy areas like airports or the downtown area of heavily populated cities, taxis are typically lined up and readily available. You need only approach one for service, which is very convenient. If you are seeking rideshare service, you must request a ride in the app and upon selection, wait for the driver to arrive at your location. In the downtown area, there are generally several rideshare vehicles already in the vicinity, but it may take a few minutes for them to get to you when there is traffic congestion. At some airports, they don't permit rideshares to pick up people in the arrival area, so you may be required to go to a different level of the airport, another side of the airport, or just outside the main airport premises. I have had this occur a few times when waiting on rideshares from the airport and metro station abroad. To me, it wasn't a big deal. I simply walked about a block over to catch my ride and was good to go. I normally have no more than a duffle bag and a medium-sized piece of luggage on wheels though. If you travel with a lot of bulky luggage, I could see where it could potentially be an issue. In this case, you may consider taking a taxi versus a rideshare.

Moreover, on the discussion of availability, when taxis are not lined up and ready to go, it can be challenging to quickly hail a cab for a ride. I have hailed cabs on different continents, and no matter how many cabs are in the area that pass by, I have rarely, if ever, been able to get service from the first one I try to flag down. In many cases, they are either already in-route with a passenger or selective about who they are responding to for rides. Whichever the situation, it can be a bit frustrating after multiple attempts. On the flipside, you don't have this concern with the rideshare. You just book your ride, and your driver comes to you.

I should mention that in order for you to use the rideshare app, you must have it downloaded on your phone and you must have Wi-Fi or data access. It could be an issue if you are in an area where there is a poor signal or limited/no coverage, such as a rural area. Of course, in a rural area, you may struggle accessing a taxi as well. You would possibly need Wi-Fi/data and phone service to search for a taxi company and to call to arrange your transportation. If you are traveling abroad, this means you would also require international phone/data service.

For riders with disabilities or who need transportation with wheelchair access, Uber presents options that cater to your needs. You are able to book UberXL or UberWAV (Wheelchair-Accessible Vehicle) rides and rest assured that the driver has the proper arrangement to accommodate you. In addition, if you or your driver has a hearing impairment, the app informs the other party after the ride has been booked, which helps minimize confusion and awkward interaction by providing the information in advance.[188] Uber's assistive technology like the vibrating alerts and the capability for riders to communicate by typing a destination and sending messages to their driver rather than speaking out loud are also pluses for passengers who are deaf or hard of hearing.[189] These options and features would definitely make someone in these applicable categories lean towards taking an Uber over a taxi.

Pricing and Payment

So, which is cheaper? Is it the taxi or the rideshare? The answer: "It depends." In most situations, the rideshare is less expensive, but this is not always the case. The primary exception occurs for short trips in major cities like New York, London, and Sydney, where taxis are everywhere and are the cheaper option. Nonetheless, for longer trips, for most rides to the airport, for regional service outside of urban centers, and in the suburbs and smaller towns, you will pay less for a rideshare than a taxi.[190]

It is important to note that fares fluctuate according to the time of day. Taxis charge by the minute when you are gridlocked in traffic, and Uber's surge pricing increases rates

---

[188] Forno, "Uber, Lyft, Grab, Taxi?"
[189] Yip and Daniels, "Uber vs. Taxi?"
[190] Ibid.

during commuting/rush hours, Friday afternoons, and whenever the bars/pubs close in the area. Surge pricing is a hike in the base price of an Uber fare computed by appraising supply (the number of drivers in an area) and demand (the number of people who need a ride). Uber's surge pricing algorithm is proprietary, but people claim that pricing can range from a normal surge price of 1.5 times the base rate up to extreme increases of three-to-four times the base rate during major holidays like New Year's Eve. Surge pricing can be very localized—literally within a few blocks—and vulnerable to changes every one hundred seconds or faster. So, if your surge pricing ever gets outrageous, you can generally outsmart the algorithm by delaying your ride by a few minutes and then resubmitting your order or by walking a few blocks away from whatever is triggering the surge near you.[191]

Popular tourist areas are often prone to surge pricing due to the ratio of potential riders gathered at these locations to the number of drivers in the area. So, if you can, avoid ordering a pickup from a highly populated tourist attraction. While it may not always be ideal to walk a few blocks, it may be worth it in order to save $50 USD or more. Though taxis do not have what is termed surge pricing, taxis in cities worldwide do modify their

---

[191] Forno.

base pricing throughout the day in a model that indistinctly resembles surge pricing.[192]

An advantage of using a rideshare is the upfront pricing. You don't have to bother with haggling for a ride, which you may have to do if taking a cab. Not to mention, in a foreign country, you may not be familiar with the language or the rules of negotiation you must engage in for a ride. It's so much more hassle-free to order a ride via an app, where you already know roughly what you will be paying and that the rate will be fair (outside of surging, of course).

Likewise, the payment process for a rideshare is a lot more straightforward and convenient than it is for a taxi. Paying via the rideshare app with the card you've already got saved prevents you from having to pull out a card or count and handle cash. Plus, you don't have to worry about struggling to come up with the exact change needed for a cash payment. On a side note, in the event you end up taking a cab and have to pay in cash or voluntarily choose to do so, make sure you pay attention to the bills you provide and what you receive in change. Some countries have bills that look very similar, and you don't want a mix-up where you pay too much or receive less back in change than you should. Also, if a driver casually claims not to have

---

[192] Ibid.

change, calmly remain in the ride, and respectfully request correct change. More than likely, when he realizes you are not falling for the scam, he will "coincidentally" be able to locate the correct change eventually so you can be on your way.

Another advantage of the rideshare payment process is that you can also easily assign how much money you would like to tip the driver in the app by selecting a percentage or cash amount to pay. As a rule of thumb, do a bit of research ahead of your trip to educate yourself on the tipping protocol of your destination to find out if it is customary to tip your driver, waiter/server, etc. and if so, what the appropriate tipping amount or percentage is. You can reference the World Factbook Travel Facts for basic tipping guidelines per country.

If you are in an area where there are several people waiting on a ride to go in the same general direction (i.e., at the airport waiting for a ride to go downtown), it can be common for people to share a cab and split the cost. This can be a good way to save money. Just so you know, you can also divide up the cost among passengers in many rideshare apps as well. For example, Uber offers UberPool, and Lyft offers LyftLine as carpooling options.

Navigation/GPS

Rideshare apps are linked with navigation support like Google Maps, so both the driver and you as a passenger are able to view directions to your requested destination via the app. This is great for a number of reasons. First of all, it prevents you from having to explain to the driver exactly where it is that you want to go and how to get there. If you are in a foreign nation or even just somewhere you have never been before, you may not be familiar enough with the area to talk through how to get to your intended destination. Additionally, if there is a language barrier, it may be difficult for you and the driver to communicate with one another. You must also keep in mind that there are some cultural tendencies that may exacerbate the situation. For instance, in some cultures, it is not favorably viewed to admit when you don't know something. So, you may have a cab driver who has no clue where it is that you want to go, let alone how to get there, and in an attempt to remain agreeable, he does not express this to you. As a result, you may end up spending valuable time (because time is literally money in this case) aimlessly riding around town.

Another benefit of utilizing a rideshare that has GPS with directions displayed through the app is that you can monitor your progress in real time and recognize right away if the driver is not following the intended route. Sometimes, taxi drivers will take the scenic route to try to rack up extra miles and, therefore, money unbeknownst to you as the passenger. Similarly, they may take you down a path with a bunch of tolls for which you are responsible for paying instead of taking you a different way that would be less expensive for you overall. The rideshare app depicts the best route based on traffic, which helps avoid unnecessarily extended and/or costly trips. On the subject of tolls, it is unfortunate that I have to say this, but I do; be sure that you verify the cost of the tolls for yourself versus just handing over the amount requested by the driver. The driver can scam cash out of you by inflating the toll cost that he/she tells you that you need to pay.

One last serious reason why it is beneficial to be in a rideshare with common GPS is that you can be aware if the driver is taking you somewhere altogether different from your requested destination. Look out for some of these potential red flags:

- The vehicle is going in the opposite direction compared to the route directions displayed in the rideshare app

- The estimated time of arrival to your destination is increasing as opposed to decreasing as you ride along (not stuck in gridlocked traffic)

- There is a drastic change in scenery or environment in comparison to the place where your ride originated when there shouldn't be

- The driver's demeanor or behavior appears suspicious, unsettling, or threatening, especially when you question him/her about the route

Some rideshare apps like Uber and Lyft have a feature where you can "Share Your Ride" with others so that they, too, can track your progress to your destination. While this is convenient in that they are able to know when you are expected to arrive, it is also helpful from a safety perspective should something go awry such as your being kidnapped or worse. They are capable of alerting the authorities to your approximate location in addition to you or in the place of you in the unfortunate event you are unable to do so yourself. This brings up another critical safety tip. In case of an emergency, ensure that you know what number to dial. As Americans, we all know to dial "9-1-1" if we need emergency assistance anywhere in the U.S. Make it part of your safety routine to know the equivalent of that number in foreign nations that you visit. This information can be found in the World Factbook Travel Facts.

If you are taking a taxi instead of a rideshare and are, therefore, not able to take advantage of the common GPS in the app, it is a good safety practice to use a map app on your phone to view directions and track your route. This way, you can still benefit from some of the same tips I have shared earlier in this section.

Safety

As I proceed on the topic of safety, I should emphasize that no method of transportation is 100 percent foolproof and perfectly safe and secure. There are risks associated with each; nevertheless, there are facts and precautions to retain.

In terms of vehicle safety, Uber and Lyft require vehicle maintenance reports from their drivers. Practically all taxi companies begin their days by inspecting their vehicles, and they are required to procure a vehicle inspection yearly in order to retain their operating permit. So, you should feel fairly safe with either the rideshare or taxi as it pertains to vehicle safety.

Lyft and Uber require background checks from their drivers, but the drivers are not regularly monitored and regulated like taxi drivers. The background checks and training required to become a rideshare driver are generally not as extensive as what is required for those seeking to become a taxi driver, plus taxis are typically regulated by the city. Numerous cities mandate that taxi drivers and limousine drivers obtain a hack license or chauffeur's license, which signifies that they have participated in many hours of classroom-style and behind-the-wheel training.[193]

Although the rideshare drivers are not monitored and regulated by the city, the apps do have a system where at the end

---

[193] Loftus. "Lyft, Uber vs Taxi."

of the ride, passengers give drivers a rating, normally between one and five stars. Simultaneously, the drivers rate the passengers. This is a way to keep both parties in check, so to speak. If drivers have a low rating, riders are less likely to select them, which directly impacts their bottom line. So, they have an incentive to provide excellent service. Some apps even require that their drivers maintain a minimum rating such as 4.6 stars out of five stars in order for them to maintain their driver status with the company. Additionally, since riders are not just rating the drivers on their safety but also their behavior and the cleanliness (or lack thereof) of their vehicle, you have a higher probability of experiencing a better encounter on the whole with a five-star-rated rideshare driver than with a random taxi driver you hail off the street. On the flipside, if riders make a habit of acting out and being a jerk to drivers, they may find themselves stranded somewhere, struggling to receive service and possibly, eventually banned from the app. So, this is a good system, given the checks and balances implemented.[194]

Over the years, there have been several high-profile cases around theft and assault involving taxi drivers throughout the world. By and large, people are inclined to believe that rideshares are the safer option; however, they have experienced their fair share of controversies as well with reports of sexual

---

[194] Corby, "Uber vs Taxi."

assault, rape, and kidnapping accusations and charges against Lyft and Uber drivers in the United States, the United Kingdom, and Australia. This goes to show that neither choice is truly completely safe, so just be vigilant and aware of the risks. Also, keep your eyes peeled for the red flags discussed in the previous section, so you are as prepared as you can be to respond accordingly.

Riders Beware

Here are a few scams and scenarios you need to be aware of if you plan on traveling via taxi or rideshare.

Drivers with Unmarked Cars / Individuals Posing as Taxi or Rideshare Drivers

NEVER EVER get into an unmarked vehicle, period.

To do so is risky and potentially very dangerous. In some countries, there are so-called taxi drivers who aggressively hound you in the baggage claim area inside the airport, trying to pressure you to take a ride with them. They insist that they are ready and eager to take you where you need to go for the best price. It is a scam! Their "taxis" are unregulated, and that means there is nothing preventing them from charging you whatever they want which can be up to three times the normal rate a regulated taxi would charge. Heaven forbid, they just outright rob you or worse.[195]

Avoid following someone out to a parking lot or garage, down an alley, or to anywhere secluded and/or not well lit. Taxi and rideshare drivers usually have to operate at marked, regulated taxi stands and pick-up areas, so it should trigger a "mental alarm" if the surroundings appear suspect or unsafe.[196]

Unfortunately, in various places, there have been cases of people posing as drivers who end up kidnapping and assaulting unsuspecting riders. The rideshare apps provide the driver's name and the color, make, model, and license plate of the vehicle. Always verify this information *before* getting inside the vehicle. When you greet the driver and attempt to validate his name, don't ask, "Are you John?" He can simply respond, "Yes" whether that is his name or not. Instead, ask, "What is your name?" This requires him to provide a name that you can then check.

Taxis with a Meter Not Running

If you are a passenger in a taxi and you notice that you have been riding along for a few minutes, but the meter is not running, it may be tempting not to say anything because you

---

[195] Forno.
[196] Ibid.

may be thinking that you are going to get a deal/steal on the ride. In fact, you should definitely say something because remaining silent could actually have the opposite effect of what you're thinking. The driver may end up charging you an absorbent amount for the ride. Let the driver know as soon as you notice the meter is not running. Taxis are legally obligated to have a visible, functioning meter. If the driver declares that the meter is damaged or, for some reason, not working, request to end the ride right away. It is a "rip-off" to have you pay a crazy amount of money.[197]

Never-ending Rideshares

Rides don't automatically end in the rideshare app when you reach your destination; they must be deliberately ended by the driver. Prior to exiting your rideshare vehicle, assert that the driver officially ends the ride in the app. Otherwise, dishonest drivers may try to rip you off by allowing the "meter" to run for miles after your ride until they pick up their next fare.[198]

Rideshare Presence throughout the World

The information provided in this section is current as of 2020. For the most up-to-date data, refer to the respective rideshare websites.

---

[197] Ibid.
[198] Ibid.

Countries with Lyft Service

Currently, Lyft is solely available in the United States and in a few areas within Canada. This consists of coverage in all fifty states and the District of Columbia in the U.S. and eleven cities in British Columbia and Ontario in Canada.[199] The access to ridesharing apps in Canada is limited because of stricter regulations.[200] Check out www.lyft.com/rider/cities for a list of the specific cities where Lyft is available.

Countries with Uber Service / Countries where Uber Is Banned

Uber is presently available in about seventy countries. It must frequently update its service map because of ongoing legal battles, protests, and buyouts from competitors like Grab in Southeast Asia and Didi in China.[201] Uber has actually been banned in Bulgaria, Hungary, and Denmark.[202] There are other countries where Uber operates in a limited capacity, as the service has been banned in numerous cities within those countries.[203] Take a look at the list provided at www.uber.com/global/en/cities/ to see if Uber is available at your travel destination.

---

[199] Lyft, "Cities."
[200] Forno.
[201] Ibid.
[202] Orton, "Where Uber Is Banned."
[203] Forno.

Countries with Grab Service

If you have never heard of Grab, then you've likely not been to Southeast Asia because they are nearly everywhere over there. In 2018, Grab bought out all of Uber's operations, making them the largest (and often only) ridesharing app in over five hundred cities in these eight Southeast Asian countries:[204]

- Cambodia

- Indonesia

- Malaysia

- Myanmar

- Philippines

- Singapore

- Thailand

- Vietnam

International Alternatives to Uber and Taxis

You have plenty of options for a ride when you travel internationally, aside from Uber and Grab. The following are some of the top ride-hailing apps worldwide.[205]

---

[204] Ibid.
[205] Ibid.

- GoJek – 207 cities across Indonesia, Singapore, Vietnam, Thailand, and the Philippines[206]

- DiDi – China, Australia, New Zealand, Mexico, Argentina, Chile, Colombia, Costa Rica, Dominican Republic, Ecuador, Panama, Peru, Russia[207]

- Ola – 250+ cities across India, Australia, New Zealand, and United Kingdom[208]

- Gett – Israel, Russia, United Kingdom, and United States[209]

- Bolt – More than 150 cities across Europe, Asia, Africa, North America, and South America[210]

- Cabify – Over eighty-five cities across Argentina, Brazil, Chile, Colombia, Ecuador, Spain, Mexico, Peru, and Uruguay[211]

- 99 – Owned by DiDi, 99 operates in several cities throughout Brazil[212]

---

[206] Gojek, "About Us: Gojek."
[207] Didi, "International Business."
[208] Ola, "About Ola."
[209] Gett, "Gett."
[210] Bolt, "Find a City."
[211] Cabify, "About Us."
[212] 99, "Cities."

Rental Cars

In the *How to Get There* section on rental cars, I covered material related to the pros and cons of renting a vehicle, basic requirements for renting a car in the United States, strategies for locating deals on rentals, and things to look out for when booking a rental car. To prevent redundancy, I will not rehash these topics in this section, but know that much of that same information applies whether you are renting a car to travel in North America or abroad. With that said, I will use this section to provide information more relevant to renting a vehicle (also known as "hiring" a vehicle in some parts of the world) outside of the United States.

Things to Consider When Determining Whether or Not to Rent a Car Abroad

These four items deal mostly with your level of comfort in driving in certain scenarios and conditions. Therefore, it is a personal decision. There is no right or wrong answer; it is about what works best for you.

1. Side of the Road They Drive On – As you may be aware, in some countries, people drive on the opposite side of the road compared to the side of the road you drive on in your home country. For some, this may seem like it's not a big deal, but for others, this can be taxing

to get used to and a bit overwhelming. Turning lanes are impacted as well as the direction of pedestrian traffic. Having driven on a particular side of the road most or all of your life, you are accustomed to looking a certain way (left or right) for oncoming traffic, so it does take some adjusting initially, but it is doable if you are up for it. You can find out what side of the road people drive on in different nations by simply doing a quick search on the internet.

2. Driving Style, Speed of Traffic, and Flow of Traffic – This category really depends on your frame of reference and experience. For example, if you are only acquainted with driving in a small town with moderate, easy-going traffic, it may be an extreme change for you to drive in a busy city filled with fast, aggressive drivers, especially if you are not as familiar with the area, signs, and traffic rules and patterns. Think of how it is in some Caribbean countries where they zoom around curves, quickly moving in and out of lanes barely dodging collisions with other vehicles or an area like downtown Shanghai where there are five, six, or more undefined (at least to the average foreign onlooker) lanes of bumper-to-bumper traffic traveling alongside casual pedestrians strolling in the street. In parts of India, drivers honk their

horns at other drivers every few seconds. This can mean that a driver is upset with another driver, or the driver can be indicating that another driver needs to speed up, or the driver may be communicating that he/she is about to pass another driver, or it can mean all three of these things at the same time or something altogether different! And all of this is happening in a matter of seconds, so you have to be able to think and respond quickly. To get a feel for what it might be like driving in an area where you've never traveled, I recommend that you seek feedback from people in your Facebook travel groups who have been to the area and driven a rental car.

3. Type of Transmission Available – In a sizable number of nations, manual transmission is the norm, and in some of these locations, the rental agencies may not carry cars with automatic transmission. This can be a barrier for you if you are incapable of, unfamiliar with, or uncomfortable driving a stick shift vehicle.

4. Environment and Terrain – It's a good idea to get a heads up of what the environment is like in the area you will be visiting if you will be driving. I've given the example of traveling in a highly populated area. Well, the flipside of this would be a rural area. In some

regions, it is very common for you to be driving on a road with people riding elephants or horses right in front of or beside you or cows, monkeys, or camels nonchalantly walking across your path as you are driving. Of course, this is quite normal to the residents of the area, but this may freak you out a little bit if this is not something to which you are acclimated. Some places may have unpaved streets, dramatically steep hills, winding roads along a snowy mountainside or ocean cliff, etc. It is helpful to know about conditions like this, as it may impact your decision as to whether or not you want to rent a car to drive in the area. You can learn about this by surfing the web for descriptions of the area or asking questions in your Facebook travel groups and receiving responses from experienced travelers.

Eligibility Requirements

Once you have decided that you would like to rent a car to drive in a foreign nation, you must make sure you meet the eligibility requirements for driving in that particular nation.

Age Parameters

Several nations have a minimum rental age requirement of twenty-five years old and a maximum age limit of seventy years old. In those nations, if your age is outside of that range, rental agencies will either refuse to rent to you or have you pay a surcharge to help offset the associated risk.

International Driver's Permit

You can check with the consulate or embassy of the country you plan to visit to find out its policies on international drivers.[213] If you are seeking to rent a car in a country that requires that you possess an International Driver's Permit (IDP), you will not be allowed to rent a car if you do not have one.[214] The rental car agency can let you know whether or not an IDP is mandatory.[215] Essentially, an IDP is a document that contains your name and photo and translates your pertinent driver information into nine different languages. It is recognized by over 150 nations.[216] An IDP is normally not mandatory in English-speaking nations because your American driver's license is generally suitable. Nevertheless, if you are planning to rent a car in a nation where an IDP is a prerequisite, you will need to present it in addition to your license from your home nation.[217]

---

[213] SmarterTravel, "International Car Rental Tips."
[214] Lisse, "Rent Car While Overseas."
[215] Zakhareuski, "International Driver's License."
[216] American Automobile Touring Alliance, "International Driving Permit."
[217] SmarterTravel.

To acquire an IDP, you have to be a permanent U.S. resident, at least eighteen years of age, and possess a driver's license that will remain valid for a minimum of six months from the issue date of the IDP.[218] You must have obtained it prior to having left your home nation, as it has to be issued by your home nation.[219] The only two agencies authorized to issue IDPs in the United States are the American Automobile Association (AAA) and the American Automobile Touring Alliance (AATA). Any other organization attempting to sell you an IDP is a phony trying to swindle you, as they are not authorized. Also, beware of companies offering to supply you with an International Driver's License that supposedly gives you more privileges, rights, benefits, or discounts than an International Driver's Permit. There is no such thing! This "license" is a hoax.[220]

In order to apply for and receive an International Driver's Permit within the same day, you can download an application from the AAA website, fill it out, and take it to your nearest AAA branch office along with two original passport-sized pictures of yourself, your valid U.S. driver's license, and a check or money order to pay the $20 USD permit fee.[221] This is the

---

[218] Ibid.
[219] Ibid.
[220] Zakhareuski.
[221] American Automobile Association.

least expensive and quickest way to attain your IDP. Otherwise, you can apply by mail via AAA or AATP. With this route, you will have to pay shipping and handling fees in addition to the permit fee. If you include postage for express mail service, you can expect delivery up to ten business days after the IDP is processed. Normal processing time is ten to fifteen business days. If you do not include the additional postage for express mail service, it may take up to four to six weeks for you to receive your IDP. An International Driver's Permit is valid for one year.[222]

Automobile Insurance

No matter where you are renting a car, you need automobile insurance coverage. Consult your auto insurance policy to ascertain whether or not your policy covers your rental car in foreign countries. More than likely, it does not. Alternatively, you can check to see if your credit card company travel coverage includes car rentals abroad. If neither of these two options works for you, then you need to find out if the rental car company offers insurance and, if so, prepare to purchase the insurance at the time of booking your reservation. You are only allowed to refuse rental coverage with proof of existing coverage. Regardless of the source from which you attain the insurance

---

[222] American Automobile Touring Alliance, "FAQ – Frequently Asked Questions."

coverage, verify that the coverage meets the minimum requirements set forth by the foreign country.[223]

Booking Your Rental Car

Plan to book your rental before your trip. By doing so, you will save yourself money and hassle. Rental rates are almost always more expensive in person at the rental counter as opposed to online or over the phone in advance, even if it is merely twenty-four hours before your time of pickup.[224] Utilize the strategies previously discussed in the *How to Get There* section of this book to locate deals, as most are applicable for domestic and international car rentals.

Although many US-based companies are represented overseas, there are some agencies that are more prevalent overseas as well as OTAs that are slanted more toward international searches. Auto Europe and Europcar are popular rental car agencies in Europe. Auto Europe is known to have low rates and outstanding customer service and are good for assisting with difficult rentals like finding a rental agency in Ireland that rents to drivers over seventy years old. While Sixt is a higher-end rental company, you can occasionally find special deals on rentals in European cities, saving you more money than you

---

[223] Lisse.
[224] SmarterTravel.

would typically discover on other sites, so be on the lookout for that.[225]

Although there are several nations in Africa where car rental is not recommended, renting a four-wheel drive (4WD) vehicle has progressively become a popular way to get around in Southern Africa, especially in Botswana, Namibia, and Zambia. Chiefly, vehicle rental in Africa is relatively expensive, as two-wheel drive vehicles normally cost over $75 USD per day in sub-Saharan Africa and 4WD vehicles run around $150 USD a day. Plus, this can be accompanied by hefty insurance fees and various restrictions. Perhaps, your best chance at a bargain is to rent a car in South Africa for an extended period of time for what can possibly cost you less than $30 USD, particularly if you book from overseas. Some vehicles can then be driven from South Africa into Namibia, Mozambique, and Botswana. Additionally, you can consider renting a car for exploring southern Morocco or venturing through wildlife parks at your leisure in Kenya and Tanzania (possibly with a driver). Note that in some places, you are unable to rent a car without a local driver being included in the deal. On the contrary, in other countries such as Botswana and Namibia, it's not possible to rent a vehicle *with* a driver. Africamper, Avis Safari Rentals, Britz, and Bushlore Africa are the names of a few companies renting

---

[225] Perkins, "Best Rental Booking Sites."

4WD vehicles in Southern Africa for journeys and self-drive safaris. If interested, check them out.[226]

International rental agencies like Avis, Hertz, and Europcar are represented in several large towns in the Middle East and in airports, capitals, and tourist hubs in Southeast Asia. Local companies generally have cheaper rates, but vehicles supplied by the international agencies are frequently better maintained and include a better backup service in the event problems arise. An advantage of patronizing local companies is that they sometimes allow you to hire a driver along with the rental car for prices comparable to renting the car by itself; it is certainly worth considering this option.[227]

Most rental companies in Southeast Asia require you to provide a deposit in order to rent a vehicle. Either you are to leave your passport with them as a security deposit or pay a substantial cash or credit card deposit.[228] Though it is okay to surrender your passport, as it would be under safe keeping, I recommend that you opt to pay a credit card deposit because you may need your passport for identification or miscellaneous other things during your trip. I choose the credit card deposit over the cash deposit because I, personally, don't like carrying a lot of

---

[226] Lonely Planet, "Africa/Practical Information."
[227] Lonely Planet, "Middle East/Practical Information."
[228] Lonely Planet, "Southeast Asia/Practical Information."

cash on me because if it is lost or stolen, it's pretty much gone and that is that. However, if my credit card is lost or stolen, I can just cancel it or put a hold on it and my credit card company will reimburse me for any fraudulent charges made on my card as a result of theft.

In many Southeastern Asian and Middle Eastern countries, it is more common for people to ride motorcycles and scooters versus driving cars. In these regions, travelers often rent a motorcycle or scooter for local transportation. Motorcycles and scooters have high availability, especially in popular tourist cities and are less expensive.[229] Also, they are easier to maneuver through traffic in town. Though a motorcycle license is not always requested by the rental companies, it is frequently a legal requirement for operating manually geared motorcycles and scooters. Renting without a valid license can result in grave consequences should you be involved in an accident or traffic infraction, so it is best to take the necessary precautions to be law-abiding.[230] Travel outside of town to other cities via rental car or motorcycle is not very widespread in the Middle East or Southeast Asia due to poor road conditions and the challenge of competing with trucks and speeding buses on national highways

---

[229] Ibid.
[230] Ibid.

in Southeast Asia. For this reason, public transportation is the recommended mode for long-distance travel in Southeast Asia.

In the Middle East and Southeast Asia, you may want to hire a driver through a local rental car company or travel agency or directly as an independent contractor. Check out reviews for drivers on Tripadvisor, and ask for recommendations on drivers from travelers in your Facebook travel groups. I have utilized both of these resources, respectively, for driver services in Thailand and India. I planned out my own itinerary, coordinated with the drivers beforehand via WhatsApp and email, and got to visit all the popular tourist sites on a budget.

Perhaps, you are looking forward to exploring some of the famous scenic routes on the well-maintained network of roads in Australia. You can rent a car, 4WD vehicle, or motorcycle from companies in the major airports or central city locations. Car rentals can be as cheap as $27 USD a day. Popular rental agencies include Alamo, Avis, Budget, East Coast Car Rentals, Enterprise, Europcar, Hertz, and Thrifty. Britz provides 4WD and campervan options for hire in Australia and New Zealand.[231] You can peruse the websites of these particular agencies or start with a travel search engine like Kayak and explore deals from there.

---

[231] CarRental.Deals, "Best Car Rental Companies in Australia."

Car rentals are available on practically all of the islands in the Caribbean. Those that don't have rentals are likely in areas where there are no roads. Some of the familiar international chains offering service in the Caribbean include Avis, Budget, Dollar, Eurocar, and Hertz. Note that several Caribbean nations drive on the left side of the road, but this varies from island to island. If you plan on renting cars on multiple islands, bear in mind that you may need to shift back and forth – physically and mentally – as you travel in order to abide by the road rules and laws of the land. You should also be aware that some cars have steering columns on the side opposite of what you may be accustomed to seeing.[232] In other words, the steering wheel is on the side that we in the U.S. would consider the passenger side of the car. This may take some getting used to, but it is manageable.

In Central America, car rentals can range anywhere from about $15 USD per day in Nicaragua to $55 USD per day in Belize and approximately $30 USD to $80 USD per day for a 4WD vehicle. The fuel and mandatory insurance costs can be a bit pricey though. You may actually come out cheaper by reserving a car in advance or even the same day via the website of an international rental chain versus renting locally due to some excessive insurance fees that get tacked onto your bill,

---

[232] Lonely Planet, "Caribbean/Practical Information."

perhaps, unnecessarily. All Central American nations drive on the right side of the road, and the roads are in relatively decent condition unless you are attempting to venture out to more secluded areas like the beaches south of Tulum, Mexico or Costa Rica's Península de Nicoya. For these types of locations, you should plan to rent a 4WD vehicle in order to approach them. It is not recommended to drive outside the main tourist areas because of poor road conditions and unusual driving habits of the locals. In locations where the roads are badly maintained, motorists drive vehicles that are in bad shape, and they tend to make up their own rules of the road. Most rental agencies will not allow you to drive the rental beyond the border of the country in which you rent; nevertheless, there are a few exceptions, as Budget will permit you to rent a car that you can drive from Guatemala to Mexico, Honduras, and El Salvador with some limitations. Scooters and larger motorcycles are available for rent in some places in Central America, and the price of the motorcycles can run about the same price as a compact car.[233]

Avis, Budget, and Hertz are some of the international chains with locations in South American capitals and airports in major cities. As is the case with many of the other areas I have discussed, you can usually find cheaper rates with the local car

---

[233] Lonely Planet, "Central America/Practical Information."

rental companies. Prices can range broadly from around $40 USD to $80 USD a day. Renting a car in South America affords you the opportunity to delve into isolated areas like the parks that are inaccessible by public transportation. For the chance to explore places such as Patagonia and other parts of Chile and Argentina, a short-term rental car can be deemed a worthwhile expense.[234]

When you book your rental online or over the phone before your trip instead of in person at the agency counter, you not only have an opportunity to get cheaper pricing, but you also often avoid policies with hidden clauses, fluctuating exchange rates, unfamiliar rental specifications, language barriers, and other cultural differences.[235] The less possible drama, the better.

Rental car classes and sizes vary across countries. For example, what Europeans may categorize as an intermediate car, we may consider a compact car in America, as European car sizes tend to run smaller than their American counterparts. Be mindful of this as you make your reservation.

As previously mentioned, in numerous countries, manual transmission is standard. Frequently, cars with automatic transmission are available; however, you will pay a premium for

---

[234] Lonely Planet, "South America/Getting Around/."
[235] SmarterTravel.

this luxury. If you can drive a stick shift, you can save money by renting a manual vehicle.

Find out about payment terms and methods. Many overseas rental agencies only accept credit card payments. Companies in some nations may require that you pay a deposit upfront before you drive off in the vehicle, and sometimes, this deposit must be paid in cash. It would be useful for you to know this kind of information ahead of time so that you can be prepared.

Be sure you understand procedures and charges around the return of the vehicle. Are you only able to return the vehicle during the company's business hours? If you are able to return the vehicle during after-hours, what is the associated process? If you rent a car on Wednesday at 9:00 AM and return it at 10:00 AM on Thursday, will you be charged for an additional hour or will you be charged for another full day? Does the car need to be returned with a full tank of gas? These are the types of questions you need to ask during booking. This way, you cut back on confusion and surprise charges after the fact.

Tips for Preparation

Before your trip, become acquainted with the rules of the road in the country you will be driving in by learning details like who has the right-of-way in a traffic circle or whether you can turn right (or left, in some countries) at a red light. You can locate this kind of information via the country's consulate or embassy resources or an up-to-date, thorough country guidebook.[236]

You should get a copy of a map of the city/region you will be visiting before you travel or immediately upon arrival. Additionally, print out a copy of directions to places you know you will be traveling to right away, such as from the airport to your hotel or from your hotel to a famous tourist attraction. You are probably accustomed to using a map app on your phone to help navigate your way from here to there. Many of these apps require Wi-Fi access which you may or may not have, depending on your cell phone plan. Furthermore, even if you have an international phone/data plan, mobile access can be questionable in some remote areas within particular countries. Under these circumstances, a map can come in handy. At the very least, you can take screenshots of maps and routes on your phone in advance so that you can refer to them later offline as needed. Of course, you can see about renting a car that has GPS. If this is a necessity for you, be sure to notify the rental agency when you make your reservation, so they can plan to have a car with GPS or an add-on GPS unit available for you when you arrive. Before you leave the rental agency, make sure the GPS is set to a language you understand if you do not know the local

---

[236] Ibid.

language.[237] Request assistance from the staff at the agency if you need help. Even with GPS, I still recommend that you have map copies or screenshots to reference as a backup. Some rental car agencies offer free maps, so be certain to take advantage of that.

Do a brief search on your internet browser to get an idea of the average cost of fuel in the area you will be visiting. Often fuel is more expensive overseas compared to gas prices in the contiguous United States. It's good for you to know approximately how much money you should plan to set aside in your trip budget for gas.[238] Plus, if you are offered the pre-paid gas option at the rental agency, you will know whether or not they are truly presenting you a deal.

---

[237] Ibid.
[238] Ibid.

STEP THREE – Plan What You Are Going to Do While There

I am big on planning, so I think it is great to have some sense of framework in terms of what you plan on doing while on your trip; however, I do believe that it is essential to leave some room for life to just happen. Some of my more memorable travel experiences were not scheduled but occurred naturally as I ventured down the unbeaten path.

So, my suggestion would be to plot out a few "must-see" places to go and "must-do" things to accomplish during your trip planning phase but leave space to add locations and activities you discover once you are there. Worst-case scenario, you end up with unplanned time that you can use for exploration, recreation, or relaxation.

Festivals, Concerts, Sporting Events, and Special Annual Events

I have grouped these events together because they have two main things in common: 1) They are date-specific and 2) They frequently draw large crowds. Because of this, it means that it may be necessary for you to make plans far in advance (i.e., months or even over a year ahead of time), depending on the popularity of the event. It may also mean that you should expect to pay a premium price on everything from parking to lodging to entertainment to shopping at the event as well as for these same items within the city away from the event venue. Many vendors count on tourists coming to town for certain events, so they raise their prices during this time due to the well-known concept of supply and demand. There is really no way to avoid this, but at least, you can anticipate it in order to ensure you accurately budget for your trip.

A Sampling of Examples

While I can't possibly name absolutely every festival, concert, or event that exists worldwide, I can provide some broad categories to help you think of some potential activities that may be of interest to you.

There are festivals around all types of music, foods, beverages, films, fashion, creative arts, literary arts, ethnicities/heritage/cultures, plants, animals, hobbies, and themes. Festivals entertain, educate, inspire, and connect people with a common interest or passion. If there is something that you deeply adore, there is bound to be a festival somewhere in the world celebrating it. Do an internet search to find your tribe. Don't be afraid to get out and explore. You'll find that you will be in good company.

After all, we're actually more alike than we are different.

In terms of concerts, the easy thing to do is to grab a tour schedule of your favorite artist, group, band, or ensemble to find out where and when he/she/they will be performing and plan accordingly. You may also look at broader searches based on a particular genre or style of music. Based on the time of year, you may be able to catch a good concert series. For instance, many large cities have outdoor summer concert series that are often free and open to the public. These may feature local artists and/or nationally or even internationally renowned artists.

There's nothing like being in a packed arena/stadium surrounded by fellow fanatics such as yourself rooting on your favorite team or player to victory. The environment is intense, thrilling, and amazing. The energy is unequivocally electrifying and contagious. The experience is unique and unforgettable. Sure, it's cool (and comfortable) to cheer for the home team in your home city, but it can also be fun to travel to an away game to support them while exploring something new and different. Whether you are driving a couple of cities over, flying across the country, or traveling to the other side of the world to attend a sporting event, it can be a good opportunity to awaken your senses to diverse sights, sounds, scents, and tastes. It is a chance to ease your way outside of your comfort zone because in the midst of the foreign surroundings, you are still able to cling to a bit of familiarity and sense of community with your fellow fans.

Look to see if your team or league has a game outside of your home country. For example, since 2007, the NFL (National Football League) has played a few American football games in the UK each year. There have also been basketball games with NBA (National Basketball Association) players hosted in South Africa. Perhaps, you are a tennis fan and may be interested in attending the U.S. Open, French Open, Australian Open, or Wimbledon. Soccer/football enthusiasts might enjoy catching a FIFA World Cup. Maybe, golf is your sport of choice, and you want to experience a PGA/LPGA Tour (United States), PGA Tour Canada, European Tour, Japan Golf Tour, or Sunshine Tour (Africa). Or, how about checking out multiple sports at a Summer or Winter Olympics? If you are simply a lover of sports and athletics in general, you don't even have to be a fan of a particular team or sport to attend a game abroad. In fact, you can learn about a sport that is altogether new to you by attending a game. It's a rather organic way to immerse yourself in a culture and fellowship with the locals.

Beyond the festivals, concerts, and sporting events, some cities have special events that take place around the same time each year. Some examples are religious observations, historical reenactments, cultural celebrations, and local/regional holiday festivities. They may be recognized in a variety of ways from solemn assemblies and customary ceremonies to parades, parties, fireworks, and live entertainment.

If your goal is to visit your travel destination specifically to attend such events, make sure you study to equip yourself with the appropriate knowledge, especially pertaining to history, culture, and religion. For certain gatherings, you may be expected to wear a specified type of garb or carry yourself in a particular manner, so you need to be familiar with the social norms and traditions and honor them. Whether you plan to actively participate, be a curious spectator, or stay as far away as you can, you should be aware of these events and know as much as you can about them in advance of your trip. Some areas of town may be shut down or unusually crowded as a result of the event. Many businesses may observe different hours of operation than they normally do. Additionally, as previously mentioned, lodging, parking, etc. may be limited and or more expensive during these times.

A Few Tips

Research the event extensively as you begin making arrangements for your trip. Be sure to read all the fine print. Recall that many charges and fees are nonrefundable, so double-check dates, times, locations, and prices before you submit payment. Retain your receipts and have copies handy to present at the event just in case something does not go according to plan and you need to show proof of registration and/or payment. Also, carry with you detailed information about the event including logistical particulars (i.e., name and address of venue, parking structure/lot or fairground name and location, stadium/arena/building/stage/hall/section names or numbers, event brochure or schedule with agenda, event contact phone number or email address). Be safe, have fun, and enjoy your event!

Tours and Exploring the City

Traveling Solo in a Group

For those of you who are hesitant to solo travel because you are nervous to travel alone, uncomfortable being by yourself, or just prefer to be among others, group tours are the way to go for you! As a solo traveler on a group tour, you get the best of both worlds. You're doing something you want to do, but you get to share the experience with others. Extroverts generally thrive in these kinds of environments, as they effortlessly mingle with people and immediately jump right into conversations. For some shy people, it may be a little unnerving striking up a conversation with a complete stranger. Well, the thing about tours, especially city tours, is that they are mainly comprised of tourists. So, an easy ice breaker is to introduce yourself and state where you are from, and people will likely reciprocate. Let the conversation flow naturally from there. Perhaps, you will meet other solo travelers you have something in common with who are interested in linking up with you for other activities after the tour. Maybe, you meet a small group of friends who invite you to join them, or you feel comfortable enough asking if they mind you joining them if you feel compelled to do so. Again, you want it to be a natural encounter. You don't want to come off as being too clingy or like you are a stalker. You should be able to sense the vibe and react fittingly. If you are not really interested in meeting or getting to know anyone, this is fine, too. Just enjoy the company of those around you for that particular tour.

City Tours

One of the best and easiest ways to get to know a city is by going on a tour. The most traditional tours are those where you have a guide who escorts you around town, explaining the history and culture of the area while highlighting popular landmarks and tourist attractions. These are nice because they serve as a great introduction to the area and give you a lay of the land. If I go on this type of tour, I like to do it within the first two days of my arrival in town. This way, after going on the tour, I feel like I know a bit about the natives and the culture, I have a frame of reference in terms of where I am located within the city, I have gotten a chance to take pictures at most of the well-known sites at the beginning of my trip, and I get ideas about places I may want to come back to and explore further at my leisure.

The mode of transportation for these types of tours may vary. They can be via van, bus, coach, car, boat, bicycle, Segway, foot, etc. Pricing can range from free up to hundreds of dollars depending on the length of the tour, destinations covered, entrance fees, mode of transportation, amenities included (e.g., air conditioning, snacks/lunch/dinner, beverages, equipment) and whether it is a public or private tour.

If you are looking to go the economical route, there are several cities that offer free public walking tours that you could join. Walking tours are good when a city has a lot of historical, cultural, and popular tourist sites centrally located in town or within reasonable proximity to one another. The guides usually really know their stuff because they've led the same tour over and over again with many tourists from all around the world asking just about every question you could imagine, so they have answers on a range of topics. In fact, at some point during the tour when the guide is not busy or immediately following the tour, I often ask the tour guide for recommendations on everything from the best places to shop for reasonably priced souvenirs and gifts to restaurants to "must-see" and "must-do" things to conquer before I leave the area. As a result, I have always received great advice and suggestions.

One thing to remember about walking tours, biking tours, and any other type of tour where you are not in or on a motorized vehicle is that you need to be in good health and relatively good shape. You do not want to put yourself or anyone else at risk if you are not physically capable of or prepared to participate. Beyond being embarrassed, you can be seriously injured which may be an even more complicated matter if you are in a foreign land and not familiar with the location, language, culture, healthcare system, etc. Pay attention to the details in the description of the tour. They will normally state the level of effort required (i.e., easy, moderate, difficult), recommended degree of experience of participants (i.e., beginner, intermediate, advanced), and average length of the tour. You know your body and its abilities/limitations; respond in kind. Aside from the risks, walking and biking tours can be a fun way to explore the city while getting some exercise and sun rays.

Food Tours

In addition to the city tours, there are a variety of themed tours you can join. A form of tourism that I see increasing in popularity is gastronomy tourism, also known as culinary tourism or food tourism. These terms are frequently used interchangeably and encompass both food and beverage. Erik Wolf, the Executive Director of the World Food Travel Association, defines food tourism as "the act of traveling for a taste of a place in order to get a sense of a place."[239] By going on a food tour, you become educated on local culinary cultures, customs, and history through the art of storytelling.[240] You could potentially visit local favorites, "hole-in-the-wall" restaurants, famous pubs, or street food stands off the main thoroughfare in order to have an authentic food and beverage experience. Satisfy your curiosity by expanding your mind and exposing your palate to new flavors, textures, cultures, and heritage.

Wine Tours

In a similar vein, let's shift our attention to tours emphasizing beverages. In areas known for their wine

---

[239] World Food Travel Association, "What Is Food Tourism?"
[240] Ibid.

production, it is very common for there to be wine tours. In the United States, there are wine tours in Sonoma and Napa Valleys in California, Willamette Valley in Oregon; Fredericksburg, Texas; and Charleston, South Carolina, to name a few. Outside America, there are some world-renowned wine tours in Hunter Valley, Australia; Alentejo, Portugal; Rioja, Spain; Bordeaux, France; Tuscany, Italy; Santorini, Greece; Maipo, Chile; and Cape Town, South Africa.[241] I participated in a magnificent day-long wine tour in Cape Town. It was all-inclusive with transportation to and from my Airbnb residence, tour guide, visits to five farms, cellar tour, all wines, cheese tastings, chocolate pairing, lunch, and local treats. All of this was for less than $45 USD!

Distillery and Brewery Tours

Continuing with the beverage tours, there are distillery and brewery tours for those who are seeking to learn about the process of making craft beer, ale, and/or whiskey and tasting some along the way. You will find tours like these in Milwaukee, Wisconsin; Denver, Colorado; Nashville, Tennessee; and Atlanta, Georgia in the U.S.A. Abroad, you can participate in tours in Prague, Czech Republic; London, England; Dublin, Ireland; and Melbourne, Australia. Brussels,

---

[241] Malathronas, "World's Best Wine Tours."

Belgium which is known for its beer, chocolate, and waffles has beer tours that also include these famous eats as well. All these tours come with a tour guide and transportation so that you can be informed and enjoy yourself while drinking responsibly.

Street Art Tours

If you enjoy art and are open to gazing at artwork outside of the traditional museum environment, you may like exploring a city through participation in a street art tour. Street art is a contemporary form of independent graffiti art with images artistically expressed in public places for viewing. Going on a street art tour is a great way to take in some beautiful sights, learn about the history and culture of an area, and listen to anecdotal tales and folklore. It is also a way to be introduced to and support local artists. I attended a street art tour in Buenos Aires, Argentina where we not only roamed the streets of the city examining unique artwork but also stopped by a small art museum and a pub to chat with one of the local artists over a snack and drinks. It was a nice touch. I also went on an amazing street art tour in Rio de Janeiro, Brazil. Our tour guide was extremely knowledgeable about the various art styles and techniques and was familiar with the local artists, their crews, and their stories behind the artwork. We walked and rode through many different areas of town, and that gave us a broader perspective of Rio. More and more cities around the world are offering street art tours nowadays. It is worth investigating.

Architecture Tours

You can learn much about a city through stories illustrated by its structures and buildings. In Bruges, Belgium, there are walking tours sharing the history of this medieval town through architecture. During tours in Abu Dhabi and Dubai in the United Arab Emirates, it is revealed how these originally small Bedouin fishing villages have been transformed through substantial architectural developments into the vibrant fast-paced urban cities they are today. In the United States, in Florida, there are tours of the Art Deco Historic District where guides use the architecture of the buildings to communicate the history of Miami Beach and its people. New Orleans, Louisiana has walking tours and horse and carriage tours through the French Quarter and Garden District where a guide uses architecture to narrate the history of the city through landmarks, homes, and cemeteries. In Illinois, there are numerous Chicago architecture tours where you get to see and learn about over forty famous buildings. These guided tours are primarily via boat – cruise boat, speedboat, kayak, etc. – on the Chicago River or Lake Michigan. Your selection of boat is fundamentally based on your desired pace and level of adventure.

Private Tours

If your budget is such that you have a bit of money to spend and you prefer more of a personal curated experience, you can go on a private tour where it is just you and the tour guide and a driver (if the guide is not driving). Private tours cost more than public group tours, but they offer more flexibility regarding the itinerary; they can be catered to your schedule and specific interests. In general, they have some set destinations and activities on the agenda as well as some optional places to visit. You are able to designate how much time you want to spend at certain locations or add/remove locations as discussed when making your reservation. When you are touring with a group, you may end up spending an hour at a place that is boring to you or feel rushed at a place that is really fascinating to you. On the set group tours, there is usually a tight schedule that the guide and driver have to follow in order to check everything off their list. The private tours are a little more relaxed.

Self-Guided Tours

Perhaps, you like the idea of exploring the city without the group but don't want to pay the cost of a private tour. Alternatively, you could utilize a rideshare service for half a day or a full day to take you to all the popular landmarks and tourist attractions. In advance of your trip, you would need to research the places that you want to visit so that you can give the list to the driver. Your research could merely consist of borrowing ideas directly from the descriptions of the group tours. This would enable you to visit the sites and take pictures. However, keep in mind that the driver is not a tour guide, so he/she will likely not be able to spew out all the facts, statistics, history, and cultural information about the area like a tour guide would, so that part of your "tour" would be deficient. If that is not of concern to you, then this arrangement is a good way to save money while checking out the major sites.

You could also do something similar to create your own self-guided themed tours. You could go online and investigate the top restaurants, wineries, and breweries in the area and journey to those destinations for your own food, wine, or brewery tours. Likewise, you could find popular areas for street art and unique architecture in the city and rent a car, take a taxi, or use a rideshare service to travel there and take pictures. Of course, it wouldn't be the same as the organized tours in that you would not have the benefit of hearing the anecdotal tales and learning facts about the associated history and culture from a qualified tour guide. Also, when you factor in the costs of transportation, larger food portions, and undiscounted samples of wine and/or beer versus the packaged deals supplied by the touring companies, you would be paying substantially more. The main two things you would stand to gain by going this route would be the freedom to pick and choose where exactly you want to go and the flexibility of scheduling when you want to go and how long you want to stay at each location. Frankly, I would recommend the company-organized tours for the structure, learning opportunity, and budget-friendly pricing.

Hop-On, Hop-Off Bus Tours

Perhaps, a compromise between a group tour and a private tour but a slight step up from a self-guided tour would be taking advantage of a hop-on, hop-off bus tour. City Sightseeing is one of the well-established companies offering this inexpensive way to explore a city while enjoying a somewhat flexible tour schedule. They exist in major cities throughout the world such as Paris, France; London, England; Rome, Italy; Barcelona, Spain; and Washington, D.C., New York City, New York; San Francisco, California; and Chicago, Illinois in the USA. I utilized them in Tokyo, Japan and Johannesburg, South Africa. It was a cheap and convenient way for me to move around town to hit up all the hot spots, sightsee, and learn the history and facts about the city while on the bus listening to recorded commentary through earphones provided by the company. So, this is how it works:[242]

- You purchase a twenty-four-hour or forty-eight-hour ticket.

- There are generally two to four routes with popular tourist attractions.

- You have unlimited access to ride the buses during operating hours for the duration based on the ticket purchased.

- A few cities offer optional routes for an additional charge, and some of these routes are via boat as opposed to bus.

- Attraction entry tickets are available in some packages, often at a discounted price.

- There is multi-lingual commentary in ten-plus languages on the bus with information about various sights as the bus proceeds through the city.

For more information, visit their website at https://www.hop-on-hop-off-bus.com/. Aside from City Sightseeing, there are other bus companies or touring companies providing a similar hop-on, hop-off bus experience. For instance,

---

[242] Hop-On, Hop-Off Bus Tours, "Bus Tours Low Prices."

in Australia, Greyhound offers hop-on, hop-off bus passes for popular routes. Busabout extends hop-on, hop-off services throughout Europe, stopping in major cities.[243] If you are interested in these types of tours, find out if any are available at your travel destination.

Sources for Tour Information and Booking

Companies like Viator and Get Your Guide have websites and apps where you can search for and purchase reasonably priced tours. For tours in Asia, Klook offers more options; they also have a website and app. Airbnb Experiences sometimes contains tours provided by hosts on the Airbnb site. Some hotels, hostels, vacation rentals, and bed and breakfast locations may be able to arrange tours for you at discounted prices if you are lodging with them. Be sure to shop around to compare prices to ensure you get the best deal. Many companies offer free cancellation if you cancel prior to twenty-four hours before the tour. In situations like this, you can always make a reservation in advance of your trip to secure a slot while you continue to look for a better bargain. For one of my trips to Mexico, I had purchased some reasonably priced tickets online prior to my trip, but once I arrived at my hotel, I discovered that they were selling tickets for nearly half the price of those listed online. I purchased

---

[243] Lonely Planet, "Europe/Getting Around/Bus."

the tickets at the hotel and then canceled the reservations I had made online for a full refund. That freed up money I was able to apply elsewhere.

Museums and Educational Activities

Whether traveling domestically or abroad, there are generally options of museums to visit and/or educational activities in which to partake. You can choose museums to visit based on your personal interests and what appeals to you. There are museums focused on art, history, natural history, science, technology, anthropology, archeology, astronautics, astronomy, religion, sports, music, and the list goes on and on. In addition to standard or traditional exhibits, some venues offer interactive or hands-on activities which can be a nice alternative.

If you like animals, plants, or nature, there are aquariums, zoos, animal sanctuaries, national parks, and botanical gardens through which you can wander. These consists of fun learning opportunities in both indoor and outdoor environments. Many of them offer guided or self-guided tours, exhibits, and educational films. If you really enjoy interacting with animals, of these options, I recommend that you consider going to an animal sanctuary. While in Thailand, I visited an elephant sanctuary where I learned about the elephants' daily regimen and participated by helping to feed them, give them a mud treatment, and bathe them. It was a cool experience. In Bali, I went to the Sacred Monkey Forest Sanctuary in Ubud where the monkeys roam freely and frolic; it was certainly an interesting and entertaining event!

Some people like to learn a new skill or build on an existing skill while they are on vacation. When I vacationed in Hawaii with a friend of mine, we took a class on how to make flower leis. In addition to learning how to do something neither of us had done before, it gave us a chance to learn a little about Hawaiian culture and flowers from our instructors. We also had the opportunity to mingle with other tourists in the class. There was a family in the class who had been on the island for a few days, and they told us about other activities they had participated in and restaurants they had dined at that they recommended. This was nice because it gave us ideas of things to do and places to go that were not on our list. A couple of days later, my friend ended up taking a scuba diving lesson that she really enjoyed. Aside from adding to her scuba diving experience, the lesson allowed her to explore the waters and see and learn about several beautiful creatures that were specific to that region of the world. I have known people to take cooking classes while on vacation. This activity is full of benefits! You are educated on something new about a different culture and cuisine with diverse seasonings and flavors, you learn how to make a new dish, and last but not least, you get to eat some amazing food. It is a win-win-win situation!

In order to find out what museums or other educational activities may be available at your travel destination, using your favorite browser, do a keyword search for your travel destination city plus the word *museum* or whatever type of activity in which you are interested. You can also perform searches at sites like Tripadvisor, where you can get ideas and suggestions along with the corresponding reviews which I recommend that you examine.

Depending on where you are lodging, there may be classes, workshops, and activities organized by the venue or arranged in coordination with other groups with which they partner. Resorts often offer enrichment programs and cruise lines have excursions and activities available, also. Additionally, Airbnb Experiences has hosts who offer a wide variety of activities and classes on everything from cooking to paddle boarding to making jewelry to beekeeping and more.

Adventurous Activities

If you are down for a good thrill or adrenaline rush, there are plenty of selections in several locations. Perhaps, you love a good rollercoaster with the exhilarating highs and sudden dramatic dips; find out if there are any amusement parks or theme parks at your travel destination. Maybe you are an animal lover who can appreciate a cross between education and adventure. Then, you should certainly consider going on a safari. These are just a couple of suggestions; the list is never-ending.

Part of the excitement in addition to experiencing the activity itself is doing it in a different environment, so it is also a form of exploration that intensifies the enjoyment. For example, when I went parasailing on Paradise Island in the Bahamas, I relished in the delight of coasting through the air, but even more, I appreciated the pleasure of doing so above the beautiful aqua blue water, white sand beach, and iconic Atlantis. What a spectacular memory!

There is a plethora of adventurous activities available worldwide. It is nearly impossible for me to name them all, but I will provide some examples to ignite your brainstorming of ideas. The activities are grouped in categories according to where they primarily take place. By no means are these lists intended to be exhaustive.

Air

- Skydiving

- Hang gliding

- Paragliding

- Hot air ballooning

- Bungee jumping

- BASE jumping

- Ziplining

- Swinging over jungles

Water

- Snorkeling

- Scuba diving

- Jet skiing

- Water skiing

- Tubing

- Wakeboarding

- Surfing

- Whitewater rafting

- Tidal bore rafting

- Paddleboarding/Stand up paddling (SUP)

- Flyboarding/Hoverboarding

- Kayaking

- Canoeing

- Swimming with sharks, dolphins, sting rays, etc.

- Cliff jumping into water

Snow/Ice

- Skiing

- Snowboarding

- Dog sledding

- Trekking

- Mountaineering

- Snowshoeing

- Ice climbing

- Ski biking

- Snow tubing

- Snowmobiling

Land

- Hiking

- Rock climbing

- Mountain climbing

- Mountaineering

- Abseiling

- Canyoning

- Caving/Spelunking

- Volcano boarding

- Volcano trekking

- Dune bashing

- Sand boarding

- Camping

- Bicycling

- Motorcycling

- Three-wheeling/Four-wheeling

- Walking across seemingly unstable bridges at tremendous heights

- Climbing extremely tall structures and landmarks

If you are intrigued by any of these activities, find out if they are available at your travel destination. Obviously, you will need to conduct thorough research and perform your due diligence to validate the history, reputation, safety, and security measures exercised by the organization facilitating these activities to confirm they are legit and up to standard. For most of these activities, you will be required to sign a waiver, so the companies will not be held liable for your injury or death. Guarantee that you have the appropriate insurance prior to your trip. The thrill is real but so is the danger. Be sure to follow all of the instructions and rules communicated to you for the safety and protection of yourself and others.

Disclaimer: Though I have participated in several of the previously listed activities, I am not endorsing any of them. If you choose to engage in these or similar activities, you are doing so voluntarily and at your own risk.

Shopping

Some people enjoy casually shopping while on vacation as a way to get out and explore the city while buying a few one-of-a-kind items to take back home as a memento of their trip. Others view shopping as the main purpose of the trip. Whether you're shopping for knick-knacks and souvenirs or planning to purchase your entire wardrobe while on vacation, I've got some great tips for you.

Planning and Preparation Prior to Your Trip

Multiple Methods of Payment

If you are planning on doing any kind of shopping while on your trip, you need to have more than one way to pay for your purchases, especially if you are shopping abroad. You should have at least two credit cards that do not charge foreign transaction fees and are from two different companies. With foreign transaction fees, you could end up paying three percent or more on top of the purchase price of your item, so you want to avoid this if at all possible. You want to travel with more than one card just in case one gets lost or stolen or if one of your banks happens to put a hold on one of your cards. You need to have cards from different companies because one merchant may accept Visa but not American Express, while another may not accept Visa or American Express but will accept MasterCard, for example.[244]

In addition to having credit cards with no foreign transaction fees, your cards should have chip and PIN (personal identification number) capability to aid in ensuring accessibility and fighting against fraud. The majority of international ticket machines require that credit/debit cards have a chip also known as EMV – Europay, MasterCard, and Visa. It is a technical

---

[244] Jet, "12 Tips Shopping Abroad."

standard devised to make sure that all microchip-embedded payment cards function with the terminals of merchants who accept them. This is done to decrease fraud so that if someone finds or steals your card, he/she cannot use it without knowing your undisclosed four-digit PIN.[245] If your current credit cards do not have chip and PIN capability and/or charge foreign transaction fees, you should strongly consider getting at least one credit card that works more in your favor.

As you research credit card alternatives, also think about acquiring a travel rewards card. Many cards allow you to earn sign-up bonuses to redeem miles and points for free flights and hotels. Several cards promote welcome offers of up to fifty thousand points when you meet their minimum spending requirement.[246] I have a travel rewards card that presented a similar offer that allowed me to apply the introductory points towards a nice international vacation, and as I use my card on everyday purchases, I earn points that can be applied toward travel credits that pay for my flights, hotel stays, shuttle transfers, rental cars, etc. As a result, I have been able to take advantage of discounted and even free trips. Again, it is certainly worth taken into consideration if you are in the market for a new credit card.

---

[245] Ibid.
[246] Nomadic Matt, "Planning Your Next Trip."

Aside from the credit cards, you should also plan to carry cash for shopping. There are some places that will not accept credit/debit cards or will require you to make a purchase of a specified minimum amount in order for them to accept a card payment. Plus, cash comes in handy when you are making small purchases anyway. Be prepared to carry a variety of notes or denominations. Some shops may not accept bills of a higher denomination, especially for small purchases. You should also only plan to pay in the local currency. As a scam, some major stores overseas ask customers if they would like to pay in their native currency. To the average naïve tourist, this would appear to be a courteous proposal and a convenient option; however, in actuality, the vendor would have the ulterior motive of charging a significantly higher exchange fee than what the customer's bank back home would charge.[247] Do not fall for this trick.

Two questions that frequently come up within travel communities are as follows: 1) When is the best time to get your foreign currency for your trip? 2) From where should you get it? I usually try to get a few hundred dollars' worth from my local bank about five days or so before my trip, but you may want to go earlier if it is a small bank that may have to acquire the cash from a larger branch. I like to have a little bit of cash, so I am not pressed to find an ATM immediately upon arrival at my

---

[247] Jet.

travel destination. Your local bank where you have an account will generally have decent exchange rates. They are definitely better than the rates you would get at an exchange area at an airport or in a tourist area at your destination country. I have typically found the best rates at ATMs at the destination, often at the airport, in a relatively obscure location. Large international airports have ATMs located in multiple places. Sometimes, those that are the most visible have slightly higher rates than the ones that are off the main path. Regardless of which machine you choose, be alert and aware of your surroundings, especially if you use the ATMs that are in the city. If I want to be super prepared, in advance of my trip, I search the website of the airport where I will be arriving to double-check that they have ATMs and find out where they are located, so I already know where to head when I land.

On the topic of ATMs, it should be noted that when you use an ATM in a foreign nation, you could be potentially charged a range of fees including a non-bank ATM usage fee, ATM operator access fees, and international transaction fees for the currency conversion. One way to minimize or avoid the non-bank ATM usage fee for each withdrawal and the ATM operator access fee is by using your ATM/debit card at an ATM that has an international partnership with your bank. You can usually find a list of these partners on your bank's website.[248] On your smart phone, take a screenshot of the logos of these partners, so you will have them to reference as you spot ATMs at your travel destination. There is a handful of banks that either offer accounts that will either waive international transaction fees or reimburse you for them if you are charged. You can perform an internet search to identify these accounts if you are interested.

I am often asked if I use a debit card to make purchases when I am traveling abroad. Personally, I seldom do because my debit card is not protected as much as my credit cards are. If my credit card is lost or stolen, I am responsible for a very minimal amount if anything at all if I am able to quickly notify my credit card company of the situation. I also have the window of sixty days to dispute a credit card charge, and in the midst of the mess, the money in my actual bank account remains untouched. This would not be the case with my debit card. The policies associated with your bank debit card(s) may be different and more favorable. In advance of an unfortunate circumstance, become familiar with the policies established at your banks and credit card companies.

---

[248] Ibid.

Bank and Credit Card Alerts

I have one last note concerning credit cards. Before you leave home for your vacation, especially if you are traveling internationally, be sure to notify your credit card company and/or bank to let them know that you will be out of the area on a trip. Supply them with locations and the corresponding dates. Some credit card companies and banks allow you the capability to do this yourself online via their website, but for others, you may have to call the companies to set up the alert. The reason why you want to inform them is that they would likely freeze your account if they were to see transactions occurring in a foreign country, suspecting that someone had hacked your account or gained illegal access to your card if you do not let them know of your travel plans in advance. Trust me, you do not want to lose access to your credit card while abroad on vacation.

Research Potential Purchases

If you are in the market for a particular expensive and/or authentic find from a specific nation such as leather goods, art, textiles, or traditional clothing, before your trip, be sure to conduct thorough research in order to ascertain what to look for and what to avoid when it comes to the type of item you are seeking. For instance, if you plan on shopping for pearls, you should know that pearls are certified and qualified in categories

A-D, with A being of the best quality. Even street vendors can certify their pearls, but you have to ask, as some will not willingly volunteer.[249] For other items, you should become familiar with marks of genuine craftsmanship and educate yourself on how to be able to spot a knock-off, so you can make your purchase with confidence. Additionally, recognize that if the "deal" you are being presented seems too good to be true, then it probably is. On the other hand, just because something is pricey does not automatically mean that it is authentic or of good quality. In summary, do your research.[250]

Getting Your Items Back Home

If you plan on doing a substantial amount of shopping during your trip, then, before your trip, you should definitely have a strategy for how you will be getting your items back home. One option is to leave some extra space in your suitcase when you pack for your trip so that you will have room to fill it with goods you acquire during your trip. This works well for small or compact goods that can be easily secured and cushioned by clothing and other soft items inside your suitcase.

Another option is to pack a foldable, lightweight duffle bag in your suitcase that you can load up with your fresh finds and

---

[249] Leposa et al., "Top Tips Shopping Abroad."
[250] Gray Malin, "Essential Rules Shopping Abroad."

bring on-board your return flight as a carry-on so that you can personally guarantee that it is handled with care. You can always check your suitcase as necessary.

A third choice is to have your goods shipped back home. You would certainly want to do this for bulky décor items for your home, artwork, or fragile items that would not be safe in a suitcase.[251] If you will be shopping in stores that offer shipping, have them ship it. For example, in Italy, many of the wineries ship the wine to the United States for a very nominal fee which prevents customers from having to lug bottles around and allows them to buy more bottles than they would be able to due to the customs restrictions on carrying wine home. (Side note: Several nations have very specific rules for how much alcohol you can bring home as well as a list of items deemed forbidden to bring. For instance, certain cheeses from the Netherlands are banned from being brought into the United States, and there are other items like meats, flowers, and plants that are prohibited. Make sure you're not breaking any rules/laws based on what you are attempting to bring back home.) If a store is able to ship your goods, it is best to pay with a credit card and attain a business card from the owner to monitor your purchases, track your

---

[251] Ibid.

package, and contact the owner should you have questions or issues at a later time.[252]

Just in case shipping is not offered at some of the stores where you will be shopping, you need to have a plan for how you will have items shipped home yourself. Get the vendors from the stores where you are purchasing the goods to provide as much dunnage, bubble wrap, cardboard, etc. as possible to help you to be able to securely package your items for shipment. Then, you can utilize the services of a company that permits you to prearrange pickup for your luggage or packages from most destinations. You are responsible for packing it up and they, in turn, pick it up and provide tracking. Luggage Free is an example of a company that offers this type of service.[253] Do an internet search for additional options, make sure to check out the reviews, and pay attention to the insurance policies. Keep in mind that international shipping can be quite costly depending on the size and weight of your package. Just as an approximation to give you an idea, a medium-to-large-sized box weighing up to thirty-five to fifty pounds would cost you nearly $300 USD.[254] So, be sure to factor in any potential added expenses for shipping to your overall trip budget.

---

[252] Leposa et al.
[253] Ibid.
[254] Luggage Free, "Price Your Next Adventure."

During Your Trip

Shopping Locations

If you are a casual shopper who mainly goes to malls and boutiques to sight-see, window shop, and/or take in the atmosphere, then you can probably achieve those goals by visiting the popular shopping areas in your travel destinations. You may also actually be able to find a nice item or two. You can generally find out about these places online in advance of your trip or through the host or staff at the place where you are lodging before or after you arrive. The truth of the matter is, however, that many of the well-known, mainstream shopping locales serve as international tourist traps that are designed with the motive of luring Americans and other travelers to purchase their mass-produced goods to take back home as though they are prized possessions.[255] Mind you, there is nothing physically wrong with the items; they are just common. If that is what you are going for, then this should be right up your alley.

If you are looking for items that are more of an exclusive nature and you are staying at a resort or a fancy hotel, they will probably have a shop onsite where you can find great one-of-a-

---

[255] Leposa et al.

kind finds. Expect the prices to be high, as you are really paying for the uniqueness of the items.[256]

Though the bustling markets can be fun, you are destined to find more special treasures if you dare to migrate off the beaten path and get the "411" from the locals. As I mentioned in the section of this book on city tours, tour guides can often give you some of the best recommendations for places to shop. Additionally, you can ask for suggestions from the bus driver, restaurant waiter/waitress, or a local you may become acquainted with while on public transport. Inquire about the location of antique shops, family-owned businesses, and other hidden gems that you may not have otherwise stumbled across on your own.[257]

Exchange Rates

I briefly touched on the importance of being conscious of exchange rates when I talked about currency in Step One of this book. Please allow me to refresh your memory. Exchange rates essentially involve how much your money is worth in one currency compared to another currency. Depending on the nation you are visiting, the divergence between currencies can vary greatly, meaning you might be overpaying (or passing up a

---

[256] Ibid.
[257] Gray Malin.

strong bargain) without even being aware of it. Before going shopping abroad, you should have a rough idea of what the conversion rate is between your home currency and your destination currency. You can always round up to the nearest U.S. dollar to make the math simpler to do in your head. In other words, if one unit of the destination currency is equal to $6.89 USD and you come across something that is ten units of the destination currency, then you know the item cost is equivalent to a little less than $70 USD without tax.

In order to generate a more precise calculation, I recommend you keep your phone handy with a currency exchange app like XE Currency while you are shopping. Also, you can use your phone to double-check prices for comparisons. If you come across something that you're having a hard time determining whether or not it is a good deal, look the item up on the web to get a feel for what the going rate might be in the area for that item or something very similar to it. Hopefully, by validating exchange rates and prices, you will reduce your probability of being bamboozled.[258] Take into account that in most situations, you are unable to return what you buy, so verify that you are making an informed decision before you hand over your cash.

---

[258] Jet.

Bartering

If you are only used to shopping in American malls and stores where prices are normally fixed and final, the concept of negotiating a price can feel somewhat "foreign" and uncomfortable. However, in numerous countries besides the U.S.A., it is quite common to haggle on the price a little; in fact, it is expected. As part of the research you do on the country before you visit, you should familiarize yourself with local customs, which should include learning about the shopping etiquette practiced in the country, so you can prepare to shop in that manner. In some nations, it may be beneficial for you to be assertive (but not rude) about what you are willing to pay. On the flip side, people in other nations may react more favorably to a more gentle and polite approach to negotiation. "Bartering can be a nuanced art, and the 'rules' can even vary within a single county."[259] Case in point, if you are in Italy, while it is totally acceptable to haggle in the street markets in Florence, it is not appropriate to negotiate at the designer shops in the Piazza del Duomo in Milan.[260]

---

[259] Gray Malin.
[260] Ibid.

Value Added Tax (VAT)

If you plan on doing some big-time shopping internationally, carry your passport with you when you shop or at least have a picture of your photo page of your passport handy on your phone to show the retailer.[261] Let the retailer know that you need the required documents to claim a refund, and the retailer will give you Value Added Tax (VAT) forms to fill out so the taxes you paid can be credited back to you. You will need to hold on to your receipts and the VAT forms and have them readily accessible along with the purchased items when you are about to leave the country at the airport, border, or port.[262] You will need to go to the VAT counter and at the airport, many of the VAT counters are before the security check points, so keep that in mind before you check in your luggage.[263] Depending on the country, you can save 15 to 25 percent with the Value Added Tax.[264]

---

[261] Leposa et al.
[262] Jet.
[263] Leposa et al.
[264] Jet.

After Your Trip

Retain Your Receipts

After you return from your trip, you should keep your receipts at least until all loose ends are tied. If you had goods shipped home that you purchased abroad, hang on to those receipts until you receive the goods and have validated that they were received in good condition. In the unfortunate instance that damage did take place in transit, it would be advantageous to have the receipt available when filing a claim.

Up to a week after you return from your trip, monitor the accounts associated with the credit, debit, and/or ATM cards you used while you were on vacation. Occasionally, somehow, your card information can be transferred to people who make charges on your account. It can occur at a business that you patronized while you were on vacation or an altogether different company that you have never heard of before but is located in the city you visited. It is helpful to have your receipts on hand to double-check against your card statements. Sometimes, the name of the business you bought something from does not exactly match the merchant's name the business uses when performing financial transactions. This is why it is helpful to reference the receipts for names, transaction dates, and prices. Note that you may need to use a currency converter to factor in the exchange rates.

Label Your Keepsakes

Many people accumulate a variety of things as souvenirs to remind themselves of the places they have been, to allow them to reflect on the experiences they have had, and/or to display them so others can see them, triggering conversation and the sharing of memories. If you collect items like refrigerator magnets or shot glasses that have the names of the places visited clearly printed on the objects, it is easy to know where you acquired them. However, if you collect items like artwork, perfumes, or jewelry and you travel a great deal, it may not be as intuitive as to where you got those items from decades after your trip. For example, I collect elephants, and I have a handful of elephants from Mexico, the Bahamas, Jamaica, and South Africa that are carved out of wood. Although they each have very distinct characteristics, years from now, it might be challenging for me to remember exactly which one came from where as I continue to amass possibly 80+ other elephants. A way to remedy this is to adhere a small label or piece of tape in an inconspicuous location on the object to help jog your memory later. The label can display an abbreviated location and date.[265] I suggest you do this soon after you return from your trip, so you don't forget.

---

[265] Leposa et al.

Nightlife

Whether you enjoy listening to the live saxophonist playing jazz in a plaza in Rome, Italy as you view artwork, or you prefer indulging in the lively bar and nightclub scene along Bangla Road in Phuket, Thailand (both of which I have done and appreciated), there is generally some form of nightlife to explore in most major cities throughout the world. There is a variety of venues where you can party, listen to great deejays or live music, dance, karaoke, laugh at comedians, watch sports on large screen TVs, play games, view performers, socialize with others, be entertained, eat, drink, smoke, and be merry. To each his/her own. You can make plans based on what you like to do and what you are looking to get into while on your trip.

Use your favorite search engine to search for keywords like nightlife, nightclubs, bars, lounges, live music, etc. paired with the name of the city you will be visiting. That should help you generate a decent list of places to examine. From there, you can find out if those places have Facebook pages where you can see pictures, videos, and reviews so you can begin to get a feel for the type of atmosphere or vibe you can anticipate as well as the kinds of crowds that frequent the venue. A lot of places will have flyers posted on their Facebook pages and/or websites so you can find out about upcoming special events. You can also see if they have certain nights designated for particular activities such as open mic night, trivia night, or ladies' night. This will be useful in terms of helping you determine which specific night(s) you want to go.

As always, you want to keep your personal safety in mind. You do not want to go somewhere that could be speculated as dangerous, especially as a solo traveler. Do your research. Look at online reviews. Get ideas, recommendations, and feedback from people in the Facebook travel groups I discussed earlier. It never hurts to ask, "Hey, has anybody been to Club XYZ in [Insert City]? If so, what was your experience like?" It can save you from a boring, uncomfortable, or even scary scenario, depending on the situation. Once you have an idea of where you will be lodging at your travel destination, you can reach out to the place to inquire about popular nightlife activities enjoyed by guests. They typically would not suggest something deemed unsafe to the general public. However, I still believe that the Facebook groups would be your best resource because you will gain more personal insight that is potentially more relevant to you specifically. Plus, their opinions are unlikely to be swayed by any type of affiliation, whereas, some hotels have partnerships with the local businesses where they get a percentage for referring patrons.

Self-care and Wellness

Self-care is about doing what makes you feel good with regard to your mind, body, and soul.

This can include engaging in physical activity, spa treatments, reflection, and refreshments.

In the mountains of Switzerland and Norway, you can take a rejuvenating hike while delighting in views of gorgeous scenic cliffs. The Netherlands, one of the most cycle-friendly nations in the world, is known to have more bicycles than residents. So, it comes as no surprise that cycling is a primary mode of transportation there. When visiting the region, be sure to leave some time to steal away from the hustle and bustle of the tourist attractions to de-stress on a casual bike ride.[266] There are countless destinations worldwide like Canada, Peru, and the U.S. where you can unplug and relish in nature escapes.[267] In the masses of state and national parks in America, relax and appreciate your natural surroundings. Across the globe, enjoy a pleasant stroll along the beach as you watch the sun set in places like Seychelles, Hawaii, Mexico, Australia, Thailand, and the

---

[266] Travel Bliss Now, "Wellness Practices Around World."
[267] Travel Bliss Now; Montell, "What 'Self-Care' Means."

U.K., just to name a few. This exercise is physically stimulating while simultaneously mentally and spiritually calming.

There are some treatments that are relatively common in most spas, and then, there are those that are unique to particular regions. Thermal baths are a normal wellness practice in many nations. Given that Hungary has over 1,000 hot springs, it is a popular scene for those seeking to take advantage of the waters with heavenly vibes and various minerals recognized for decreasing blood pressure, reducing joint pain, and fostering total health. The Blue Lagoon in Iceland is a spring mixed with freshwater and seawater, containing silica that helps exfoliate and strengthen the skin. Being in it gives one a feeling of utter tranquility. Perhaps, not as well-known, thermal waters exist throughout Italy. This is especially the case in Tuscany[268]. When I learned about the Japanese bathhouses called onsens as I was planning my trip to Tokyo a few years ago, I added it to my list. I chose to visit a wellness center on the day of my trip when there was dreary weather because I knew I didn't want to be out in the rain and depressing dark clouds. Nevertheless, I did not intend on being there nearly six hours! After soaking in the onsen, I had a Shiatsu massage, and then settled down in the sauna. Following a shower, I went to a private zen room with views of perfectly manicured bonsai trees and rock formations

---

[268] Ibid.

and then rested in a relaxation room. With the dim lights and soothing sounds, I fell asleep in a cozy, plush reclining chair. To date, the time spent in that facility was one of the most peaceful, relaxing, and magical experiences I have had in my life. I left there feeling like an entirely different person. It was as if I had undergone a complete and much-needed reset.

Although you can get a Thai massage in the States, it is an absolute must that you experience an authentic Thai massage while in Thailand (and India, where it originated)[269], right? I've had several abroad that were amazing and very inexpensive compared to what I've paid in America. Services were so cheap in Bali that I had some type of treatment every day, including a facial and four-hand massage. Flower baths are also popular in Bali not only because they are exhilarating and comforting but possess a medicinal value as well. For example, dandelions aid in skin revitalization, rose petals hydrate your skin, and lavender flowers alleviate stress.[270]

The chocolate spa treatment is another one proven to carry medicinal benefits, as the cocoa in chocolate acts as an antioxidant that advances heart health, lowers blood pressure and cholesterol, and decreases stress. If this massage with chocolate

---

[269] Stanborough, "Benefits of Thai Massage."
[270] Travel Bliss Now.

sounds appealing, you should book an appointment the next time you're in Vienna, Austria.[271]

In Chile, they not only drink wine, but they bathe in it. Studies have revealed that wine baths help improve blood circulation. Additionally, Chilean women blend red grapes into a paste to use for face masks. Red grapes are rich in Vitamin C and other antioxidants that assist in skin repair leading to healthy, glowing skin. [272]

Visiting a hammam is a prevalent self-care activity in Morocco. You start out in a steam room where you are cleansed and then exfoliated and massaged. This is said to be a brilliant purification and healing of the mind, body, and soul.[273]

Meditation retreats are growing more widespread as they offer a chance to withdraw from hectic and demanding lives to pursue guidance, inspiration, peace, and harmony. Some of these programs can take place over the course of a day or last for a week or more. According to Forbes[274], some of the best meditation retreats in the world are located in the following destinations:

- Ontario, Canada

---

[271] Ibid.
[272] Ibid.
[273] Ibid.
[274] Porter, "Best Meditation Retreats."

- Bali, Indonesia

- Portugal

- India

- Stockbridge, Massachusetts (USA)

- Hawaii (USA)

A few key components associated with wellness are your mental, social, and emotional health and diet. For solo travelers who don't like being alone and/or are concerned about experiencing feelings of loneliness, in addition to participating in group tours and activities (reference those listed earlier in Step Three) and lodging in places with or among others (see Step Four), you can hang out in places where the natives socialize and partake of local refreshments. In England, it is common to pause from the stress of the day for a cup of English tea with milk and a biscuit.[275] Sweden has taken its love for coffee and culturally elevated it through Fika. This is when you not only have a coffee break but more importantly use the time to reflect on how grateful you are for the good things in life. It does wonders for your mood because it encourages a positive mindset and gives you a chance to try a tasty treat surrounded by others with whom you may mingle. For your Fika in Stockholm, consider pairing

---

[275] Montell, "What 'Self-Care' Means."

your coffee with delicious cardamom buns. Mate tea is an herbal tea famous in Argentina. This caffeine-rich drink is made primarily from a South American plant named yerba mate. Mate tea is served in a hollow gourd and sipped through a metal straw called a bombilla. It is full of antioxidants that can increase your metabolism, improve digestion, and strengthen your immune system. Argentinians regard drinking mate tea as a social event where people gather to build friendships, so don't be shy.[276]

---

[276] Travel Bliss Now.

STEP FOUR – Choose Where You Are Going to Stay While There

"The great advantage of a hotel is that it is a refuge from home life."

– George Bernard Shaw

O f course, if you're going on a cruise, where you are going to stay is one less thing you have to plan, since it is already included. For most other scenarios though, you will need to choose where you will lodge. There are several factors that weigh in on your decision of where to stay. Cost, convenience, amenities, location, safety, personal preference, comfort level, degree of interaction with others, goal of your trip, proximity to planned activities, and amount of time you plan on spending in your place of lodging are all things you need to take into consideration when selecting where you want to stay.

In this section, I am highlighting five of the most popular options for lodging. There can be a somewhat broad range in pricing within each of these categories, but I am starting out with the options that tend to traditionally be more expensive and offer more amenities and then proceeding with those that are typically less expensive and potentially delivering fewer amenities.

Resorts

There are all-inclusive resorts and those that are not. This section focuses solely on all-inclusive resorts because they tend to be the more popular option of the two, and they lean towards being more financially beneficial if you are going to go the resort route.

Perhaps, one of the best ways to gain an understanding about resorts is to contrast them with hotels.

"While hotels offer a place to stay when you're away from home, resorts are meant to be a home away from home."[277]

Resorts and hotels cater to two different demographics. Hotels are targeted at a variety of traveler types – business people, tourists, and visiting family, to name a few. These kinds

---

[277] Hakutizwi, "Hotels vs. Resorts."

of travelers do not intend on spending much time at the hotel. On the contrary, resorts appeal to vacationers who do not view lodging as an afterthought but the main attraction of their stay and the primary purpose of their vacation.[278]

Consider resorts as exaggerated hotels. A hotel may have a pool, whereas, a resort may have three pools. Similarly, a decent hotel may have an onsite fitness center, but a resort may have the fitness center *plus* a spa.[279] One of the major priorities of an all-inclusive resort is to have absolutely everything you desire and more so that you have no reason whatsoever to leave the premises. There are amenities like drinks, fine dining, shopping, and nightlife. Outdoor recreation equipment such as kayaks, paddleboards, and snorkel gear are also included. A number of scheduled activities are also available such as cooking and Spanish lessons, archery and fitness classes, and water polo and aqua aerobics in the pool. Evening entertainment may consist of performances by tribute bands, magic shows, and stand-up comedy. Although a great hotel may extend some of these types of amenities, it is typically for an added fee or the overall nightly rate is significantly more than what you would be charged at a

---

[278] Ibid.
[279] Ibid.

resort, and the assortment of activities and entertainment is not as comprehensive.[280]

It should be noted that the value of lodging at a resort diminishes significantly the more often you leave the resort to do things offsite. Given that your food, drinks, and entertainment are included at the resort, if you go out to dinner at a restaurant in town and then to a nightclub where you order drinks, you're essentially adding charges to a bill that you had already paid. With that said, if your travel goals are more geared towards exploring the city and/or experiencing activities, nightlife, and other entertainment outside of your place of lodging, then a resort is probably not the best option for you financially. On the other hand, if you enjoy the convenience of having all of the amenities you could ever want in one location and not have to keep counting your coins for every cocktail you drink, then an all-inclusive resort seems like it would be a no-brainer for you. You are generally going to pay more staying at a resort than a standard hotel, but as long as you take full advantage of all it has to offer, your luxurious resort experience will be memorable and worthwhile.

If you belong to any hotel rewards clubs like IHG (InterContinental Hotels Group) Rewards Club, Hilton Honors,

---

[280] Grant, "Resort Price Breakdown."

or Marriott Rewards, you may be able to find some special deals on their respective resorts and make reservations through them. At the very least, you can use points you have earned from past stays towards future vacations. If you do not belong to any of these types of clubs, it is to your advantage to join as soon as possible. They are free and the points accumulate relatively quickly if you travel a lot for business or pleasure. You can also search for resorts to book on websites like Expedia, Travelocity, and Booking.com. Peruse the guest reviews and ratings to acquire feedback based on previous guests' stays.

Hotels

The word "hotel" can be traced back to the 1600s with its French origin, *hôtel*. That word, like its English equivalent, referred to "a place that provides lodging, meals, entertainment, and other services to travelers."[281] While these staples represent the foundation for hotels even today, it must be communicated that not all hotels are created equal.

Hotel Star Rating System

The United States and the majority of other countries in the world use a hotel star rating system that maxes out at five stars. Let's dig a little deeper into the American system. The star

---

[281] Jones, "Hotel and a Motel."

rating system was fashioned to measure the quality of hotels as a basis for comparison. Since the number of stars allocated to hotels in some countries are assigned by local government agencies and independent organizations, the ratings tend to be slightly more consistent than those in the U.S. which are awarded by "a variety of different groups from travel guidebooks and national consumer travel associations to travel agencies and websites."[282] This is why, in America, the same hotel can be listed as a four-star hotel on one website, five-star hotel on another website, and a three-star hotel on yet another site. If you want to know what a particular rating equates to for a specific travel website or association, refer to the guide that they likely supply displaying criteria aligned with their personal hotel star rating system. For a more generic overview of each rating, here is the rundown.[283]

One-Star Rating

Though what may come to mind when you think of a one-star hotel is some seedy "hole-in-the- wall" joint, this is not necessarily the case. A one-star hotel merely designates that it is an economy/budget hotel that offers basic accommodations with

---

[282] Bell, "Hotel Star System."
[283] Ibid.

limited amenities. They have no restaurants on site, but there is normally one located within walking distance.[284]

Two-Star Rating

A two-star hotel is thought to be a value hotel. While it offers simple accommodations like a one-star hotel, it differs in that it is usually part of a larger chain or franchise rather than being individually owned (e.g., Econo Lodge or Days Inn). The rooms include a television and phone and there is frequently a restaurant or dining area on site. There is also daily housekeeping and twenty-four-hour front desk service.[285]

Three-Star Rating

A three-star rating reflects a quality hotel belonging to a larger, more upscale chain of hotels like Marriott, Radisson, and DoubleTree. They typically consist of more style and comfort and a broader range of services and amenities than what would normally be experienced at a one- or two-star hotel. You should expect a fitness center, pool, business services, on-site restaurant, room service, conference rooms, and valet services. As you may suspect based on some of these amenities, three-star hotels are geared toward business travelers. The guest rooms are

---

[284] Ibid.
[285] Ibid.

larger with contemporary furnishings and extras like flat-screen televisions with extended cable. This category of hotel is often located near a major expressway and local attraction.[286]

Four-Star Rating

Four-star hotels have lobbies complete with upscale décor and conversation areas.[287] The onsite restaurant offers fine dining and there is lighter fare served in the lounge.[288] Guest rooms are comprised of large queen or king beds with lavish bedding, pillow-top mattresses, extra seating, state-of-the-art electronic devices, mini-bars, name-brand bath products, hair dryer, and high-quality towels.[289] Amenities and services include a concierge to assist with making reservations and getting tickets, above average front desk service, valet service, poolside food service and multiple pools, hot tubs, day spa, high-class fitness center, bellhops, room service, child-care services, and limousine services.[290]

Five-Star Rating

Five-star hotels are deemed the most luxurious hotels in the world. They boast extravagant lobbies with cutting-edge

---

[286] Ibid.
[287] Anderson, "4-Star & 5-Star Hotel?"
[288] Chi, "4 Star Hotel Requirements."
[289] Anderson; Chi.
[290] Chi; Bell; Anderson."

architecture and interior design, original artwork, opulent furnishings, and fresh flowers.[291] Guest rooms are elegant and glamorous with premium linens, electronic drapery controls, large-screen plasma television with high-definition cable and surround sound, DVD player, oversized marble or granite bathrooms, double vanities, personal Jacuzzi tub, and lavish bath products.[292] The unrivaled service of staff going above and beyond with upgraded check-in services, using the guests' names and anticipating each guest's needs with the assistance of a personal butler or designated concierge.[293] Most five-star hotels offer gourmet restaurants, onsite entertainment, state-of-the-art health clubs and fitness centers, multiple heated pools and hot tubs, deluxe spa services, tennis courts, and golf course access.[294]

Hotel vs. Motel

Though some people use the words interchangeably, hotels and motels are not the same thing. As previously mentioned, the term "hotel" dates back to the 1600s and originated in France. The word "motel" came about in the 1920s and is exclusively an American lodging option. As a combination of the words "hotel"

---

[291] Bell; Anderson.
[292] Ibid.
[293] Anderson.
[294] Bell; Anderson.

and "motor," the concept of the motel was derived as America's major highway system developed and there was a need to have roadside stops available for motorists traveling cross-country. For this reason, motels are catered towards travelers who plan on having a one- to two-night stop along a journey, whereas, hotels are geared for longer stays. While hotels generally have lobbies and guests enter their rooms from the inside of the hotel, guests are more likely to access their motel room door directly from the parking lot.[295]

From a safety perspective, as a solo female traveler, I am often leery of staying in motels, particularly if the location seems a bit sketchy. The possibility that strangers can come right up to my motel room door from the parking lot makes me uncomfortable. I feel like there is at least an added layer of security with hotels given that visitors must enter the property and pass by the front desk staff and security cameras to approach the interior rooms. At a minimum, this weeds out some potential intruders who are not willing to boldly risk being discovered and/or caught.

Concerning cost, hotels tend to be more expensive as a whole, but characteristics such as property size, popularity, and location factor more into the cost rather than the motel-vs.-hotel

---

[295] Jones, "Hotel and a Motel."

designation. In summary, your decision to stay in a hotel or motel should be dependent on the objective of your trip.

If you want the place where you lodge to be just as integral to your travel experience as anything else, you should choose to go with the hotel. If you simply need a place to shower and sleep, a motel may be the better option for you.[296]

Selection Tips

If you are a platinum or black card carrier and you want to live it up like those on *Lifestyles of the Rich and Famous*, I say go for it and enjoy the five-star hotel. Otherwise, your decision should be based on your trip occasion, personal needs, and budget. There is a substantial difference between a four-star hotel and a five-star hotel, but the variation between a three-star hotel and a four-star hotel can often be very subtle to the average guest. When choosing your hotel, reflect on how much time you plan on spending in the hotel during your trip. If you are going to be out and about exploring the area and will have limited time in the hotel to take advantage of numerous amenities, it may be

---

[296] Jones.

in your best financial interest to reserve a room at a three-star hotel.[297]

When searching for hotels online, I recommend that you utilize sites that scour through several hotel sites at once. For instance, you can use Trivago, Booking.com, Expedia, and Travelocity. Look at guest reviews and ratings to get candid feedback on previous guests' experiences.

Bed and Breakfasts

There are those who may wonder, "Just what is a bed and breakfast?" Well, it can be viewed as a cross between a luxury hotel and a private home. Because of this, some may regard it as being the best of both worlds, so to speak. Typically, a bed and breakfast, or B&B, is a small establishment comprised of four to ten guest rooms as opposed to the fifty to one hundred or more found at most hotels.[298] The rooms can range from cozy to luxurious and are individually decorated with their own exclusive character and theme.[299] Most B&Bs allow you to book your specific room of choice instead of selecting a room type like you would at a hotel. Many B&Bs take pride in a very fascinating or unique history. For example, in France you can

---

[297] Cutolo, "Real Difference Between Hotel."
[298] Entrepreneur, "Start Bed and Breakfast."
[299] Superpages, "Benefits Bed and Breakfast."

stay in authentic chateaus, and in Morocco, you can stay in former palaces called riads.[300]

The owners, or innkeepers, of the bed and breakfast live on site and interact with travelers as though they were invited guests in their home.[301] This is conveyed through the personal touches such as leaving out fresh warm cookies and stocked snacks in common areas for guests, a wine and hors d'oeuvres hour in the evening, a free DVD library for in-room watching of movies, turndown service, and baskets of bath and beauty products set out on Jacuzzi tubs.[302]

It should be noted that while B&Bs offer amenities that are often not available at most hotels, there are some amenities that are offered at some hotels that are not available at B&Bs. For example, it is not common for bed and breakfasts to have a fitness center on site.[303] If you've got a routine workout regimen that is crucial to you, this may factor into your decision of whether or not you want to stay at a bed and breakfast. Of course, the specific amenities offered vary from one B&B to the next, so you must research what is offered at the ones you are considering.

---

[300] Vrbo, "Why Stay at B&B?"
[301] Entrepreneur.
[302] Entrepreneur; Vrbo.
[303] Select Registry, "Pros and Cons Bed Breakfast?"

There is one amenity that is provided at every B&B – breakfast, hence the second "B" in B&B. Every morning, you can look forward to a hot, delicious home-cooked meal. Though several hotels now serve complimentary breakfast, it is normally the same few items repeated day after day. At a bed and breakfast, the innkeepers possess the resources and ability to cook something new and flavorful each morning. Also, if you have any allergies or dietary restrictions, you can inform your innkeepers in advance, and they will be pleased to accommodate you. Most of the time, breakfast is provided to all travelers at the same time in a common space in the B&B; however, if you prefer to have breakfast alone in your room, some properties offer this option for an added fee.[304]

Bed and breakfast establishments don't typically cater to families. In fact, they tend to be popular among couples. So, if you are seeking a relatively quiet environment, a bed and breakfast may be appealing to you as a solo traveler. With fewer people and less going on, the owners are inclined to be able to keep a much better eye on the property versus the common staff at a hotel.[305] This, perhaps, may give you more of a sense of security.

---

[304] Ibid.
[305] Superpages.

Also, since there are minimal guests, the owner can provide more personal assistance and attention than what you would generally get at a hotel. They are practically your concierge and are, therefore, invested in making sure you have an enjoyable stay.[306] They can share local advice on just about anything you need to know as a traveler to a new place. This covers everything from giving restaurant recommendations to letting you know the best spots to watch the sunset. Some B&Bs extend activities such as crafting or tours of local attractions.[307] Several present recreational activities in their regular packages. Depending on the location, you may be able to take part in bicycling, hiking, canoeing, golfing, or skiing.[308]

While there are those of you who enjoy the personal attention of the innkeeper and the opportunity to mingle with other travelers, there are some of you who would rather keep to yourselves. Given the close quarters of a B&B, you may not experience the level of privacy, anonymity, and detachment that you would at a hotel or larger establishment. A lot of times, this is a matter of personal preference or personality – introvert versus extrovert. Or, it may be dependent on the goal or intention of your trip. If you're going out of town for a weekend escape where you just want to relax in peace and solitude, you

---

[306] Vrbo.
[307] Select Registry.
[308] Superpages.

may not feel like being bothered with chatty people in the hallways or at breakfast. In fact, you may feel a bit restricted by having a scheduled time for breakfast or other activities should you decide to participate. If you are somewhat of a free spirit, you may have a similar sentiment. On the flipside, if you are traveling solo and don't really want to be alone or you are a social butterfly who enjoys meeting new people, a B&B could be a good place to make acquaintances and maybe link up with other travelers you can explore the area with together. You may also appreciate the structure of having scheduled activities in order to help plan out your day.[309]

Though bed and breakfasts are frequently more expensively priced than hotels, they generally offer a better overall value.[310] If you are interested in staying at a bed and breakfast, there are two websites with a broad selection that you can peruse. They are as follows:

- Bed & Breakfast Inns – https://www.bbonline.com/

- Select Registry, Distinguished Inns of North America – https://selectregistry.com/

---

[309] Select Registry.
[310] Superpages.

Vacation Rentals

When planning a vacation, many people choose to stay in a one-of-a-kind short-term vacation rental as opposed to staying in a standard hotel. These properties include options like "uniquely-themed homes, beachfront cottages, cozy cabins, upscale condos, as well as other fun, exciting, and affordable options."[311] People primarily report that the main reasons they opt for staying in a short-term vacation rental over a standard hotel are "cost savings, additional space, and pet friendliness (when desired)."[312] Additionally, they enjoy the conveniences of having a kitchen and washer/dryer, and for those in larger families or groups, multiple bedrooms and bathrooms. Lastly, some people express that they prefer the feeling of "living locally," for unlike hotels, the rentals are spread spontaneously throughout local neighborhoods and communities.[313]

Airbnb vs. Vrbo

First of all, since I just covered B&Bs in the previous section of this book, I feel obligated to point out that, despite its name, Airbnb is considered a short-term vacation rental company and NOT a bed and breakfast. While a few properties

---

[311] Jen, "VRBO vs. AirBnb."
[312] Ibid.
[313] Ibid.

may possess some of the characteristics of a B&B, by and large, most properties do not.

The companies Airbnb and Vrbo (formerly VRBO/ HomeAway) have practically become synonymous with the short-tern vacation rental industry. Though Airbnb, founded in 2008, is significantly younger than VRBO, which has been in business since 1995, Airbnb is a formidable competitor. According to statistics currently posted on Airbnb's website in 2020, they offer over seven million accommodations located across one hundred thousand cities in 220-plus countries and regions. VRBO stands for Vacation Rental by Owner and was acquired by HomeAway in 2006. Expedia bought HomeAway in 2015 and rebranded it as Vrbo (pronounced VER-bo) in 2019 mostly for brand recognition purposes.[314] As of April 2019, Vrbo boasts over two million rentals in more than 190 countries. Let's explore some of the similarities and differences between these top two online vacation rental companies.

Both have websites and apps that serve as a platform for hosts to lease out their homes or living spaces for guests to rent by booking an online reservation. They also have in common a secure online messaging system for guests and hosts to communicate, so prospective guests can ask the host questions

---

[314] Hawkins, "HomeAway, Rebranding as Vrbo."

prior to securing a reservation. Neither platform permits potential guests to call or email a host prior to reservation confirmation.[315]

Vrbo and Airbnb allow hosts to charge a cleaning fee at their discretion. These fees assist hosts with cleaning expenses and preparation between guests' stays. Vrbo has a strict policy where the host is required to plainly display the cleaning fee on the property listing page. It is listed as a separate charge from the price per night, but it is presented upfront. Airbnb differs in that they display their price per night without indicating whether or not a cleaning fee is rolled into that price. Guests do not discover what the cleaning fee is until checkout. The downside to this is that you may be excited when you initially find a place you really like that is listed as $100/night only to be disappointed at checkout when it ends up being $150/night with the cleaning fee factored into the price. Also, the accumulation of the cleaning fee contributes to the service fee, which inflates the overall price even more. Airbnb normally charges guests a service fee of 5-20 percent of the reservation subtotal. When booking via Vrbo, guests are charged a six to 12 percent service fee of the total reservation cost minus taxes.[316] The moral of the story is that

---

[315] Jen.
[316] Ibid.

you need to view the final pricing on reservations so that you are employing apples-to-apples comparisons before booking.

Perhaps, the biggest differentiator between Airbnb and Vrbo is that Airbnb lists shared spaces, whereas, Vrbo concentrates exclusively on renting out entire houses, condos, or apartments. This is part of the reason why Airbnb has substantially more listings than Vrbo. Examples of a shared space would be the basement or spare room in someone's home. No doubt, that type of arrangement lacks the level of privacy one would have staying in a full-property rental, but travelers who are willing to exchange shared amenities for a reduced nightly rate may prefer this option. Also related to rental type differences, Airbnb is known for having some really unique offerings such as tiny houses, castles, treehouses, yurts, and even private islands. It is infrequent for Vrbo or other competitors to offer these one-of-a-kind sorts of properties. Travelers seeking more traditional vacation destinations are drawn to sites like Vrbo because of their huge inventories in popular tourist destinations. So, according to the type of experience you are seeking, you may lean toward one company over another.

Airbnb and Vrbo differ when it comes to special features each offers. As alluded to in Step Three of this book, Airbnb offers what they call *Airbnb Experiences* where you can select from a variety of activities to reserve through an Airbnb host.

Note that you can sign up for an experience with any host. It does not have to be with the host you are renting from, nor do you even have to be staying in a rental to book an experience. A special feature that Vrbo provides is a wide-ranging search filter to aid in narrowing down properties for selection. Another feature called Trip Boards allows you to assemble collections of your favorite Vrbo properties, so you can save, organize, and compare the homes you find appealing. Subsequently, you can invite members of your family or travel party to save homes, vote, and comment on your trip board.

Selection Experience and Tips

Personally, I have stayed in short-term vacation rentals all over the world and have had nothing but positive experiences. Two of my favorites just happen to be Airbnb properties. The first was a family compound homestay in Bali, Indonesia. My hosts were a nice young married couple who lived on the premises in the main house with a toddler daughter and elderly family members. I stayed in one of the two guesthouses they were renting out across the beautiful, flourishing courtyard opposite the main house. It was an upstairs unit with a cozy bedroom with a queen-sized bed, nightstands with lamps on each side of the bed, a sofa, dresser and chair, large bathroom with rain shower, and a balcony overlooking the courtyard. It included free Wi-Fi and a complimentary homemade breakfast every morning delivered by the wife to the balcony. Each evening, I would let one of the hosts know which of the four breakfast options I wanted and at what time I would like to eat the next morning. The price for everything including taxes and fees was less than $24 USD per night! For a minimal fee, the husband picked me up from the airport to bring me to the homestay and after my stay, he drove me a few towns over and dropped me off for the next leg of my vacation. He also arranged tours and cultural activities for me in town for very inexpensive prices. He had a previous career in the hospitality industry, so he had lots of connections and experience. The homestay was located within walking distance of restaurants, spas, and tourist attractions. For venues that were a bit farther out, my hosts provided complimentary moped rides and I would take a taxi back when I was ready to return. All of these benefits factored into my decision for selecting this property.

My second favorite vacation rental was a private room in a house with my hosts in Sydney, Australia. I was not originally seeking to lodge in a private room, as I typically rent out the entire place, especially when I have a lengthy stay. Nevertheless, I had my heart set on staying in a certain area of town, and none of the hosts in that area were offering full-property rentals. There were also no hotels in the area, so that was not an option either. So, once it became apparent that I would likely be staying in a private room, I filtered my search such that I was only looking at rentals with Superhosts, which are experienced hosts who have high ratings. Next, I homed in on the host profiles to get a feel for whether or not I thought we would be a good fit. I took into account people's profession, hobbies, interests, and personality when trying to determine compatibility, and I also relied heavily on reviews from previous guests. I wanted an environment where I felt comfortable and safe and I had the flexibility to pretty much come and go as I pleased. I should remark that most of the rentals were around the same price – a reasonable price – so price was not a key deciding factor. I ended up selecting a rental that was right in the suburb that I wanted. I was within walking distance of a vibrant bohemian area full of cafés, restaurants, pubs/bars, parks, and spas. You could hear live music in the streets all day and night and see jovial people strolling about from here to there. It was a great vibe. The rental was near two bus stops and up the street from a train station, so I could travel to any other major area of town with ease. My hosts had given me a metro card that already had some money on it, so I didn't have to purchase a card; I just kept refilling that card as needed. The rental was like a small townhome. My private room was cozy and suitable with a comfortable double bed, closet, bureau, and bookshelf. In the room, the hosts had provided towels, linens, toiletries, and a personal welcome note with a bottle of red wine, which were nice touches. My hosts, a young couple, were friendly and very hospitable. They gave me restaurant recommendations and excellent directions to places I wanted to go; it was helpful to know which buses and trains to take to various destinations. We also had interesting, casual conversations on the days when our paths crossed. They were both working professionals, so they would be up early and gone for the day before I even got out of bed each morning. I would explore the city during the day and hang out late at night, so they would often be in bed by the time I returned to the house. The private room was on the opposite side of the house from my hosts' bedroom. In between the bedrooms was a living room, kitchen, breakfast area, and bathroom that we shared. Given our schedules, we were each able to maintain a fair amount of privacy. One evening during the weekend, they had a small gathering of friends over for drinks and hors d'oeuvres. They let me know that I was welcome to join if I desired, and I did spend some time with them, which was nice. It was a very eclectic group. We talked about everything from educational systems, to history, to politics, to pop culture. It was a thought-provoking, informative, and entertaining discussion. Overall, I had a very favorable experience at my Airbnb in Sydney.

I would like to share a few tips so you, too, can select great vacation rentals and have memorable, positive experiences. On the various vacation rental websites or apps such as Airbnb or

Vrbo, enter your specific travel dates to get accurate pricing and availability. As previously discussed, prices vary per season, so if you just look at pricing for random dates, it may be totally different from what you would see for your actual vacation dates. The dates will also impact the results you will receive regarding availability. It would be discouraging to find the "perfect" place only to realize that it is not vacant during the dates you need.

As the results are displayed for the dates you entered, pay attention to the map that shows where the properties are located and their associated prices. Based on the activities you identified in Step Three, decide on a general area of town that is centrally located near most of the places you plan to go. This will permit you to maximize your time during your trip by not wasting a lot of time in transit traveling between activities. Use the zoom feature on the map to zoom in or out, which will decrease or increase your options, respectively. Observe landmarks and street names on the map to use as a frame of reference for your activities as well as to help make you aware of venues and establishments in the area. For instance, if you want to be near a beach, park, coffee shop, gym, nightclub, restaurants, bars, spas, etc., you should be able to check for those things on the map and detect their proximity to potential rentals.

Utilize the search filters to home in on properties with your preferred features or amenities, keeping in mind your specific situation. For example, if you are traveling with a pet, you need to indicate that you are looking for a property that is pet friendly. If you will have a car while you are in town, make sure that the property either offers onsite parking or that there is parking available nearby and find out if there is a fee associated. When vacationing internationally, don't assume that amenities that are common in the United States are standard everywhere. Be sure to document whether or not the accommodations include things like a television, satellite/cable, internet/Wi-Fi, and air conditioning if they are important to you. There are two other items you should strongly consider incorporating in your filters. The first is the Superhost badge on Airbnb or Premier Partner badge on Vrbo. I mentioned the Superhost designation earlier; the Premier Partner badge is basically Vrbo's equivalent, where the term is awarded to owners and property managers with consistently high guest reviews and low cancellation rates.[317] Speaking of cancellation, the second item you should contemplate including in your filters is free cancellation on Vrbo or cancellation flexibility on Airbnb. You definitely want to select this if your plans are not yet solidified at the time of

---

[317] Jen, "Best VRBO Rentals."

booking, but it can also be helpful to have should your plans change unexpectedly.

You can glean a great deal from the reviews written by previous house guests about their stay, so take advantage of the information. I recommend choosing a vacation rental that averages at least four stars on a five-star scale, which is 80 percent out of 100 percent. Additionally, the more reviews available on a listing, the better because this means that the listing has been rented out over a longer period of time, and the owners/hosts have a higher probability of having worked out the kinks. Ensure that you look at most, if not all reviews and that they include a variety – good, bad, old, and recent. Although some people are extremely hard to satisfy, you should not overlook the harsh reviews, as there may be a hint of validity that can give you a glimpse of possible issues.[318]

Although Airbnb and Vrbo are the most popular vacation rentals, don't feel as though you are limited to searching only their sites.

Agoda has agodaHomes, which is their own proprietary homestay service, and Booking.com has an extensive offering of vacation rentals worth perusing. When I was vacationing in Rio

---

[318] Ibid.

de Janeiro, Brazil, I stayed in an apartment that I found on Booking.com for about half the price that the hotels in the area were charging, and it was within walking distance of two famous beaches. Google Flights has a vacation rentals option as part of its search engine that is also rather impressive. The search results include properties from Vrbo, Booking.com, and several others. Plus, the results are displayed in a list accompanied by a handy price map, visually depicting the location of the properties along with their associated rental cost. So, keep Agoda, Booking.com, and Google Flights in mind, especially if you are searching for and/or booking your flights through them. It can be convenient to go ahead and grab a great deal on a vacation rental from the same website. Lastly, Trivago, which is primarily known as a site for searching hotels, presents several options for vacation rentals to choose from, too. So, their site is worthy of scanning as well.

Happy hunting!

Hostels

So, now we wrap up the lodging list with the lowest-cost option. A hostel is an inexpensive, dormitory-style accommodation, typically with a shared living space, kitchen, bed area, and a few bathrooms.[319] The shared sleeping area is

---

[319] Huynh, "Hostel versus a Hotel."

often comprised of bunk beds in a room with as few as two beds and upwards of twenty beds. There are some facilities that offer private and semiprivate rooms for a higher price; however, those with the standard arrangement propose the most affordable option with prices as cheap as $15 USD per night, even in some of the world's most popular destinations.[320] Though hostels are most common in Europe, they exist all through Asia and the Americas, too. They characteristically appeal to students, backpackers, and travelers on a limited budget.[321]

The most obvious benefit of staying in a hostel is the low pricing, but two prevalent pros for solo travelers is the opportunity to mingle with other people from around the world and possibly connect with new travel partners with whom to share the travel experience. Also, some hostels supply fun activities and entertainment for guests like games, quizzes, movie nights, and free tours.[322]

A likely disadvantage of staying in a hostel with the wide-open, shared sleeping arrangement is the lack of privacy. Furthermore, there may be security concerns if lockers are not provided for personal items. In addition, if you are the type who may want to sleep in late or go to bed early during your stay, you

---

[320] Huynh; Hartwyk, "Staying in a Hostel."
[321] Hartwyk.
[322] Ibid.

may have issues with other guests who are noisy and/or on a different schedule than you, disturbing your sleeping pattern. It should be reiterated that there are hostels that offer private rooms at a higher price, and even with the increase, they are still cheaper than the average hotel stay. While it is nice to have a shared kitchen as a place to cook and interact with others, it can be annoying if others use dishes and appliances without cleaning up behind themselves, leaving you to clean up or work around their mess. This is another potential downside of lodging in a hostel.[323]

I can share two very distinct experiences I have had staying in hostels. The first was in Paris, France when I was visiting as an exchange student in high school. My classmates and I arrived in the evening and were greeted by the manager in the lobby where she welcomed us and rattled off a list of rules, including a designated curfew, lights-out time, and quiet time. I shared a sleeping area with three other young ladies. There were two single beds and two bunk beds. There was no television or alarm clock. We had a very small bathroom just big enough for a toilet and a shower. There was a sink in the area just outside the bathroom near the sleeping area. Two of my three roommates I had known for years, and the third I had met a few days prior. Since we were all part of the same group, we were on the same

---

[323] Ibid.

schedule. We went on tours and explored the city during the day and stayed up talking and laughing each night up until the designated hostel quiet time. We ate out, so we did not utilize the shared kitchen and dining areas. Not all of the sleeping areas in the hostel had a private bathroom with them. Some shared a community bathroom down the hallway from the sleeping quarters. The location of the hostel was right in the city, so we could walk to many of the major tourist sites, which was very convenient. Nonetheless, at night, we definitely had to be careful and alert, as we had to walk through a back alley to return to the hostel. All in all, it was a decent experience. I will say though, it did make a difference that I was familiar with the people I was staying with beforehand. I was not concerned about my personal safety or the security of my personal items, and I enjoyed the camaraderie.

My most recent hostel stay was about two years ago as I was traveling solo in Bangkok, Thailand on vacation. When I had planned the trip, I originally wanted to spend four nights in a particular hotel located in the heart of the city, but it was only available for the first three nights I was in town. So, I decided to book those three nights at the hotel and book an alternate location for the last night. I wanted to stay in a totally different area of town so that I could have an assorted view and be exposed to a diverse vibe. I ended up choosing the hostel because it was contemporary, had private rooms available, possessed great reviews online, and offered a free shuttle to the airport that was less than five miles away. I had heard how crazy the traffic was in Bangkok (and saw firsthand while I was there) and didn't want to take a chance at missing my 6 AM flight the following morning. Not to mention, the price was super cheap, but the prices overall in Bangkok were relatively reasonable anyway. The hostel wasn't in a location where it really felt safe to do much walking around at night, but there was a cozy restaurant just up the street that was recommended by the person who checked me in at the hostel. I enjoyed the warm environment, great food, and live music. There was no curfew at this hostel. I had been given an access code that allowed me to unlock the front door when I returned. The lights were out in all the common areas, and the building was silent as a whole. My spacious private room on the second floor had a full-sized bed, television with basic cable, a small refrigerator with complimentary bottled water, an air conditioning unit, table, chair, and a place for me to store my luggage and hang up my clothes. The bathroom in the unit was a decent size and had a shower, toilet, sink, mirror, and blow dryer. The hostel provided towels and basic toiletries. The staff was helpful and friendly. Since my stay was short, I didn't really get the chance to interact much with the other guests. I casually spoke to the guests who were in the common area when I first checked into the hostel. I didn't really see anyone else after that. I noticed a few glassed-in rooms with multiple beds in them as I made my way to my private room. This hostel was nicer and more modern than the hostel I stayed at in France. The environment was a bit more relaxed as well, given I was not initially greeted with a list of rules or a curfew. The two overall experiences were practically night and day. I am glad I selected this option for my last night in Bangkok.

If you are interested in staying in a hostel, do your research. Learn as much as you can about the area surrounding the property, sleeping arrangements available; layout in terms of bathrooms, kitchen, lounges, and other common areas; amenities, rules/curfew, and activities extended. You can do this by utilizing Google Maps to view the surrounding area around the address of the hostel, checking out the hostel's website for information and pictures, reading reviews from previous guests, and/or reaching out to the hostel directly via email or phone call to have any lingering questions answered. You can search for hostels at these sites:

- Hostel World – https://www.hostelworld.com/

- Hostel Bookers – https://www.hostelbookers.com/

- Booking.com – https://www.booking.com/

Conclusion

Back in 2008, I took my first solo trip overseas. Oddly enough, it didn't start out as a solo trip. A friend of mine and I were planning to go to Italy to celebrate one of my milestone birthdays. I had already traveled to several countries in Europe with friends but never to Italy and certainly not by myself. My friend hadn't been to Italy before either. She belonged to a travel club and was actually the one planning the trip for us. Long story short, she ended up having to cancel at the last minute in order to help care for a family member who had suddenly gotten ill. It was an unplanned and unfortunate circumstance. I had a decision to make: Was I going to cancel as well or take over and try to plan the trip myself?

I decided to go, and I'm glad I did. Was I nervous? Absolutely! I wasn't sure exactly what to expect as a Black female traveling alone in a foreign country I had never been to before, but my intrigue and excitement allowed me to press past my fear.

Now, fast-forward to 2020. Since that solo trip to Europe, I have also traveled solo to Asia, Australia, Africa, South America, and Antarctica, visiting several countries. Sometimes, all it requires is taking that first step outside of your comfort zone in order to gain the self-assurance you need to achieve what life has in store for you.

As you have read this book, you have learned how to decide where and when to go, determine how to get there and get around while there, plan what to do while there, and choose where to stay while there. I have shared with you numerous tips and advice throughout this guide in order to equip, encourage, and empower you to successfully plan a safe solo trip anywhere in the world. You have received money-saving hacks and strategies on how to formulate travel arrangements within your budget. Without a doubt, you have everything you need to charge forward with confidence as you conquer all of your goals as a travel champion. So, with that said, what are you waiting for?!

Bibliography

"10 Of the Best Free Language Learning Apps to Download." HelloTech. As of May 14, 2019. https://www.hellotech .com/blog/10-best-free-language-learning-apps.

"12 Best Cruises for First Timers." Cruise Critic. Updated March 4, 2020. https://www.cruisecritic.com/articles.cfm ?ID=129.

"About Ola." Ola. Accessed October 17, 2020. https://www .olacabs.com/about.html.

"About Us." Cabify. Accessed October 17, 2020. https://cabify .com/en/about-us.

"About Us: Gojek." Gojek. Accessed October 7, 2020. https:// www.gojek.com/sg/about/.

"Africa/Practical Information/Transport/Getting Around." Lonely Planet. August 8, 2019. https://www.lonelyplanet .com/africa/narratives/practical-information/transport /getting-around.

"Airport Shuttle Service." GO Airport Shuttle. GO Group, LLC. Accessed August 29, 2020. https://goairportshuttle.com /airport-shuttle.

Alice. "Megabus vs Greyhound | Bus Travel across the US." *Take Your Bag* (blog). Written January 29, 2020. https:// takeyourbag.org/megabus-greyhound-bus-travel-across-the -us/.

Alton, Larry. "5 Scientifically Proven Health Benefits of Traveling Abroad." Updated May 19, 2017. https://www

.nbcnews.com/better/wellness/5-scientifically-proven
-health-benefits-traveling-abroad-n759631.

"Amtrak Routes and Destinations." Amtrak. Accessed August
29, 2020. https://www.amtrak.com/routes.html.

Anderson, Caryn. "What Is the Difference Between a 4-Star & a
5-Star Hotel?" As of June 27, 2020. https://traveltips
.usatoday.com/difference-between-4star-5star-hotel
-100879.html.

Andrews, Avital. "The Best Websites to Book Your Cruise."
SmarterTravel, As of May 8, 2019. https://www
.smartertravel.com/best-sites-to-book-a-cruise/.

"Apply for a Passport Card." U.S. Department of State – Bureau
of Consular Affairs. Accessed May 3, 2020. https://
travel.state. gov/content/travel/en/passports/need-passport
/card.html.

"Apply in Person." U.S. Department of State – Bureau of
Consular Affairs. Accessed May 23, 2020. https://travel
.state.gov/content/travel/en/passports/need-passport/apply
-in-person.html.

"Australia/Practical Information/Transport/Getting Around."
Lonely Planet. Accessed December 9, 2020. https://www
.lonelyplanet.com/australia/narratives/practical
-information/transport/getting-around/.

"A Beginner's Guide to Train Travel in Europe." The Man in
Seat 61. Accessed January 20, 2021. https://www.seat61
.com/european-train-travel.htm.

"A Beginner's Guide to Train Travel in the USA." The Man in Seat 61. Accessed August 26, 2020. https://www.seat61 .com/UnitedStates.htm.

Bell, Amy. "Navigating The Hotel Star System." Updated January 31, 2020. https://www.investopedia.com/financial -edge/0410/navigating-the-hotel-star-system.aspx.

"Best Car Rental Companies in Australia." CarRental.Deals. Accessed January 16, 2021. https://carrental.deals/blog /best-car-rental-companies-in-australia/#/searchcars.

"Best Cruise Lines for the Money." U.S. News & World Report. Accessed August 3, 2021. https://travel.usnews.com /cruises/best-cruise-lines-for-the -money/.

"Book Airport Shuttle Service." AirportShuttles.com. Accessed August 29, 2020. https://www.airportshuttles.com/.

"Book Hop On Hop Off Bus Tours at Low Prices." Hop-On, Hop-Off Bus Tours. Accessed August 7, 2020. https:// www.hop-on-hop-off-bus.com/.

Bortz, Daniel and Susannah Snider. "7 Insider Secrets to Booking Cheap Airfare." As of March 14, 2019. https:// money.usnews.com/money/personal-finance/spending /articles/insider-secrets-to-booking-cheap-airfare.

Bramblett, Reid. "The 10 Best (and Worst) Airfare Search Sites for 2020." Accessed August 22, 2020. https://www .frommers.com/slideshows/848046-the-10-best-and-worst -airfare-search-sites-for-2021.

Brown, Shelby. "Best Language Learning Apps of 2020." As of April 9, 2020. https://www.cnet.com/news/best-language .-learning-apps-of-2020-update/.

Busbud. "Everything about Bus in Southern Africa." *Busbud Blog*. Accessed November 6, 2020. https://www.busbud .com/blog/5-things-you-should-know-when-taking-the-bus -in-southern-africa/.

"Canada/Practical Information/Transport/Getting Around." Lonely Planet. Accessed December 13, 2020. https://www .lonelyplanet.com/canada/narratives/practical-information /transport/getting-around.

"Can You Take an Avis Rental Car to Mexico or Canada?" Avis Rent a Car. Accessed September 2, 2020. https://www .avis.com/en/help/usa-faqs/driving-to-mexico -canada.

"Car Rental – All You Need to Know for Renting a Car in the US." Just Landed. Accessed September 1, 2020. https:// www.justlanded.com/english/United-States/Articles /Travel-Leisure/Car-Rental.

"Caribbean/Practical Information/Transport/Getting Around." Lonely Planet. Accessed November 14, 2020. https://www .lonelyplanet.com/caribbean/narratives/practical -information/transport/getting-around.

"Central America/Practical Information/Transport/Getting Around." Lonely Planet. Accessed August 3, 2020. https://www.lonelyplanet.com/central-america/narratives /practical-information/transport/getting-around.

Chi, J.D. "4 Star Hotel Requirements." Last modified June 27, 2020. https://traveltips.usatoday.com/4-star-hotel -requirements-20482.html.

"China/Practical Information/Transport/Getting Around/Train." Lonely Planet. Accessed January 20, 2021. https://www .lonelyplanet.com/china/narratives/practical-information /transport/getting-around/train.

"Choose from More than 80 Locations Worldwide."
SuperShuttle. Accessed August 29, 2020. https://www
.supershuttle.com/locations/.

"Cities." 99. Accessed October 7, 2020. https://99app.com
/sobre-a-99/cidades/.

"Coach Travel." The Aussie Specialist Program. Accessed
October 1, 2020. https://www.aussiespecialist.com
/en/sales-resources/fact-sheets-overview/coach-tours-and
-travel.html.

Corby, Stephen. "Uber vs Taxi." October 31, 2017. https://www
.carsguide.com.au/car-news/taxi-vs-uber-30943.

Coyle, Meghan. "The Best Days to Book a Flight and When to
Fly." August 29, 2019. https://www.nerdwallet.com
/article/travel/best-days-book-flight-fly.

Crislip, Kathleen. The 5 Best Currency Converter Apps of 2020.
As of November 15, 2019. https://www.tripsavvy.com/top
-currency-calculators-3150158.

Cruise Critic Staff. "What to Expect on a Cruise: How to Choose
a Cruise." Cruise Critic. Updated January 8, 2020. https://
www.cruisecritic.com/articles.cfm?ID=1803.

Cutolo, Morgan. "The Real Difference Between a Four-Star and
Five-Star Hotel." Updated September 26, 2019. https://
www.rd.com/article/four-star-vs-five-star-hotel/.

"Dollar Car Rental Policies." Dollar Car Rental. Accessed
September 5, 2020. https://www.dollar.com/Help/FAQs
/DollarCarRentalPolicies.aspx.

"Driving Across the U.S. Border Into Canada."
VroomVroomVroom Pty Ltd. Accessed September 4,

2020. https://www.vroomvroomvroom.com/rental
-information/crossing-canadian-border/.

"Driving Rental Car to Canada or Mexico." Alamo. Accessed
September 4, 2020. https://www.alamo.com/en/customer
-support/car-rental-faqs/driving-cross-border.html.

Dunbar, Brian. "What's the Difference Between Weather and
Climate?" Published February 1, 2005; updated August 7,
2017. https://www.nasa.gov/mission_pages/noaa-n/climate
/climate_weather.html.

Elliott, Christopher. "How Is an Airbnb Different from a B&B?
Which Is Better for Your Vacation?" January 24, 2020.
https://www.usatoday.com/story/travel/hotels/2020/01/24
/airbnb-vs-b-b-whats-difference-and-which-is-better-for
-you/4552257002/.

Enterprise Rent-A-Car. "Driving My Rental Car to Mexico and
Canada." Can You Take a Rental Car to Mexico or
Canada? | Enterprise Rent-A-Car. Accessed September 4,
2020. https://www.enterprise.com/en/help/faqs/driving
-rental-car-to-mexico-and-canada.html.

"Europe/Practical Information/Transport/Getting Around."
Lonely Planet. Accessed December 6, 2020. https://www
.lonelyplanet.com/europe/narratives/practical-information
/transport/getting-around.

"Europe/Practical Information/Transport/Getting Around/Bus."
Lonely Planet. Accessed December 6, 2020. https://www
.lonelyplanet.com/europe/narratives/practical.-information
/transport/getting-around/bus.

Falzon, Edward. "Where Are the World's Best Metro Systems?"
Published July 12, 2017. https://www.cnn.com/travel
/article/world-best-metro-systems/index.html.

"FAQ – Frequently Asked Questions." American Automobile Touring Alliance. Accessed October 19, 2020. http://aataidp.com/faq/.

"Find a City." Bolt. Accessed October 17, 2020. https://bolt.eu/en/cities/.

Fisher, Stacy. "The 6 Best Free Language Learning Apps of 2020." As of May 5, 2020. https://www.lifewire.com/the-7-best-free-language-learning-apps-1357060?print.

Forno, Shawn. "Uber, Lyft, Grab, or a Local Taxi? Which Is the Best Option for Travel?" *Tortuga* (blog). Accessed September 14, 2020. https://blog.tortugabackpacks.com/uber-vs-lyft/.

Fried, Lani. "11 Of the Best Train Apps for Android and IOS." April 12, 2020; first published in 2019. https://toomanyadapters.com/best-train-apps/.

"Get a price for your next adventure." Luggage Free. Accessed July 30, 2020. https://www.app.luggagefree.com/pricing/.

"Gett." Gett. Accessed October 7, 2020. https://gett.com/intl.

Glaser, Susan. "Greyhound or Megabus? Comparison of Bus Companies in Cleveland Reveals Pluses, Minuses and Dirty Bathrooms." Posted May 29, 2014; updated January 12, 2019. https://www.cleveland.com/travel/2014/05/greyhound_or _megabus_comparing.html.

"Navigating Metro Stations Like a Pro." Go-today. As of February 8, 2018. https://blog.go-today.com/travel-tips/navigating-metro-stations/.

Golden, Fran. "How to Save Money on a Carnival Cruise." Updated October 10, 2019. https://www.cruisecritic .com/articles.cfm?ID=4380.

Golden, Fran. "How to Save Money on a Royal Caribbean Cruise." Updated October 10, 2019. https://www .cruisecritic.com/articles.cfm?ID=4346.

Grant, Lara. "All-Inclusive vs. Non-All-Inclusive Resort Price Breakdown." January 20, 2020. https://www.oyster .com/articles/all-inclusive-vs-non-all-inclusive -resort-price -breakdown/.

Hakutizwi, Bruce. "Hotels vs. Resorts–What's the Difference?" September 27, 2018. https://www.nuwireinvestor.com /hotels-vs-resorts-whats-difference/.

Hartwyk, Cait, "The Pros and Cons of Staying in a Hostel," As of January 6, 2018, https://www.passporthealthusa.com /2018/01/the-pros-and -cons-of-staying-in-a-hostel/.

Hawkins, Lori. "HomeAway, the World's Largest Vacation Rental Site, Is Rebranding Itself as Vrbo." Posted and updated May 3, 2019. https://www.statesman.com/news /20190503/homeaway-worlds-largest-vacation-rental-site -is-rebranding-itself-as-vrbo.

Holzhauer, Brett. "The Top 5 Flight Search Engines of 2020." As of June 15, 2020. https://www.valuepenguin.com /travel/best-flight-search-engines.

"Homepage." Brightline. Accessed August 29, 2020. https://www.gobrightline.com/homepage.

"How to Start a Bed and Breakfast." Entrepreneur. Accessed June 28, 2020. https://www.entrepreneur.com/article /83704.

"How to Travel Europe by Bus." The Backpacking Site. Accessed December 6, 2020. https://www.the -backpacking-site.com/transport/europe-by-bus/.

"How to Use a Eurail Pass." The Man in Seat 61. Accessed October 1, 2020. https://www.seat61.com/Railpass-and -Eurail-pass-guide.htm.

Huynh, Claudia Marie. "The Pros and Cons of Staying in a Hostel versus a Hotel." *The Daily Californian Travel Blog*. Last modified January 19, 2018. https://www.dailycal .org/2018/01/19/pros-cons-staying-hostel-versus-hotel/.

"India International Travel Information." U.S. Department of State – Bureau of Consular Affairs. Accessed May 23, 2020. https://travel.state.gov/content/travel/en /international-travel/International-Travel-Country -Information -Pages/India.html.

"International Business." Didi. Accessed October 7, 2020. https://www.didiglobal.com/international-business.

"International Car Rental Tips." SmarterTravel. June 19, 2017. https://www.smartertravel.com/international-car-rental -tips/.

"International Driving Permit." American Automobile Touring Alliance. Accessed October 19, 2020. http://aataidp.com/.

"International Driving Permit." American Automobile Association. Accessed October 19, 2020. https://www .aaa.com/vacation/idpf.html.

Jen. "5 Tips to Choose the Best VRBO Rentals for Your Next Vacation." Travel with a Plan. Last modified September 24, 2019. https://travelwithaplan.com/tips-choose-best -vrbo-rentals-vacation/.

Jen. "7 Differences Between VRBO vs. Airbnb: A Full Comparison." Travel with a Plan. September 19, 2019. https://travelwithaplan.com/7-differences-between-airbnb-and-vrbo-a-full-comparison/.

Jennings, Allyson. "Transport Tips: How to Get Around Buenos Aires Safely." April 8, 2019. https://www.worldnomads.com/travel-safety/south -america/argentina/travel-safely-buenos-aires.

Jet, Johnny. "12 Tips for Shopping Abroad." *Johnny Jet: Simplifying Travel* (blog). November 14, 2016. https://www.johnnyjet.com/12-tips-for-shopping-abroad/.

Jo. "How to Use Metro Trains in Europe." *frugal first class travel* (blog), July 30, 2016. https://frugalfirstclasstravel.com/2016/07/30/how-to-use-metro-trains-europe/.

Jones, Meghan. "This Is the Difference Between a Hotel and a Motel." Updated February 13, 2019. https://www.rd.com/article/motel-vs-hotel/.

Keyes, Scott. "How to Use Google Flights to Find Cheap Flights." *Scott's Cheap Flights* (blog). As of September 3, 2020. https://scottscheapflights.com/guides/how-to-use -google-flights.

"Know Before You Go Cruising." TravelOnline. Accessed August 3, 2020. https://www.travelonline.com/cruises /information/know-before-you-go.html.

Kwan, Tang Wai. "A Beginner's Guide to the Metro Systems in European Cities." April 2, 2018. https://www.tripzilla.com /beginners-guide-metro-systems -european-cities/76260.

Lederman, Samantha. "Greyhound vs. Megabus: Which Company Is Best for Your Travel Needs?" November 28,

2016. https://www.theodysseyonline.com/greyhound-vs
-megabus.

Leposa, Adam, David Moseder, Ruthanne Terrero, and Matt
Turner. "Top Tips for Shopping Abroad." March 3, 2019.
https://www.travelagentcentral.com/tours/top-tips-for
-shopping-abroad.

Lisse, Jamie. "How to Rent a Car While Overseas." Last
modified March 21, 2018. https://traveltips.usatoday
.com/rent-car-overseas-24479.html.

Loftus, Laura. "Top 5 Issues When Choosing Lyft or Uber vs
Taxi." *American Business Insurance Services* (blog).
December 5, 2018. https://abiweb.com/info/lyft-uber-vs
-taxi/.

Lyft, Inc. "Cities." Lyft. Accessed October 7, 2020. https://
www.lyft.com/rider/cities.

"Madagascar International Travel Information," U.S.
Department of State – Bureau of Consular Affairs.
Accessed May 23, 2020. https://travel.state.gov/content
/travel/en/international-travel/International-Travel-Country
-Information-Pages/Madagascar.html.

Malathronas, John. "World's Best Wine Tours and Trails."
Updated March 11, 2017. https://www.cnn.com/travel
/article/wine-trail-destinations/index.html.

Marshall, Adam. "The Best VPN Service 2021." Accessed
January 20, 2021. https://www.techradar.com/vpn/best
-vpn.

McLaughlin, Molly. "Getting Around Sydney: Guide to Public
Transportation." Written December 16, 2019. https://

www.tripsavvy.com/sydney-public-transportation
-4768593.

"Metro of Recife." Recife metro map, Brazil. Accessed January
25, 2021. https://mapa-metro.com/en/brazil/recife/recife
-metro-map.htm.

"Mexico Insurance." Dollar Car Rental. Accessed September 5,
2020. https://www.dollar.com/TravelCenter/TravelTools
/MexicoInsurance.aspx.

"Mexico Insurance." Thrifty. Accessed September 5, 2020.
https://www.thrifty.com/TravelCenter/TravelTools/Mexico
Insurance.aspx.

"Mexico Travel Insurance." Hertz. Accessed September 5, 2020.
https://www.hertz.com/rentacar/productservice/index.jsp
?targetPage=mexico_insurance.jsp&leftNavUserSelection
=globNav_3_5_1&selectedRegion=United+States.

Michael. "Can You Drive a Rental Car into Mexico?"
AutoSlash. Updated on March 5, 2020. https://www
.autoslash.com/blog-and-tips/posts/crossing-the-border
-from-the-united-states-to-mexico.

"Middle East/Practical Information/Transport/Getting Around/."
Lonely Planet. Accessed August 8, 2019. https://www
.lonelyplanet.com/middle-east/narratives/practical
-information/transport/getting-around/.

Mitchell, Rebecca. "How to Navigate Public Transport in
Australia." June 20, 2018. https://theculturetrip
.com/pacific/australia/articles/how-to-navigate-public
-transport -in-australia/.

Montell, Amanda. "A Fascinating Look at What 'Self-Care' Means Around the World." Updated July 24, 2019. https://www.byrdie.com/self-care-ideas-around-the-world.

Nomadic Matt. "18 Easy Steps for Planning Your Next Trip." *Nomadic Matt* (blog). Last updated February 24, 2020. https://www.nomadicmatt.com/travel-blogs/planning-a -trip/.

Nomadic Matt. "How to Travel Around Africa." *Nomadic Matt* (blog). February 2, 2020. https://www.nomadicmatt.com /travel-blogs/how-to-travel-africa/.

Orton, Toby. "7 Places Around the World Where Uber Is Banned." July 18, 2018. https://www.oyster.com/articles /where-is-uber-banned-around-the-world/.

"Out of Office: 7 Essential Rules for Shopping Abroad." Gray Malin. Accessed July 30, 2020. https://www.graymalin .com/lifestyle/7-essential-rules-for-shopping-abroad.

Payless Car Rental. "FAQ about Rental Policies." Payless Rent a Car. Accessed September 7, 2020. https://www.paylesscar .com/en/customer-service/faq/global/rental-policies.

"Payment of Exit Tax." U.S. Embassy in Costa Rica. December 2, 2013. https://cr.usembassy.gov/u-s-citizen-services /payment-exit-tax/#:~:text=Costa%20Rica%20charges %20a%20%24%8%20exit%20tax%20for%20land %20border%20crossings.

Perkins, Ed. "The 16 Best Car Rental Booking Sites for 2020." January 16, 2020. https://www.smartertravel.com/best-car -rental-booking-sites/.

Poelzl, Volker. "Overland Travel in Central America: Tips for Independent Travelers." Transitions Abroad. As of January

29, 2021. https://www.transitionsabroad.com/listings
/travel/articles/overland_travel_in_central_america.shtml.

Porter, Miriam. "The Best Meditation Retreats in The World."
November 8, 2019. https://www.forbes.com/sites
/miriamporter/2019/11/08/the-best-meditation-retreats-in
-the-world-2019/?sh=49a3bd6e6dd6.

PoundSterling LIVE. British Pound to US Dollar Spot Exchange
Rate for 1999 from the Bank of England. As of May 17,
2020. https://www.pounsterlinglive.com/.

PoundSterling LIVE. US Dollar to Spanish Peseta Spot
Exchange Rate for 1999 from the Bank of England. As of
May 17, 2020. https://www.pounsterlinglive.com/.

"Practical Facts: Using Shanghai's Metro." Context Travel.
Published February 15, 2019; updated on August 1, 2019.
https://www.contexttravel.com/blog/articles/practical
-facts-using-shanghais-metro.

"Renew my Passport." U.S. Department of State – Bureau of
Consular Affairs. Accessed May 23, 2020. https://
travel.state.gov/content/travel/en/passports/have
-passport/renew.html.

Rhodes, Elizabeth. "Where U.S. Citizens Can Travel Without a
Visa." Updated December 20, 2020. https://www
.travelandleisure.com/travel-tips/customs-immigration
/where-us-citizens-can-travel-without-visas.

Rodgers, Greg. "7 Reasons Traveling Is Good for the Mind and
Body." Updated August 14, 2019. https://www.tripsavvy
.com/how-travel-will-enhance-your -life-1458533.

Rodgers, Greg. "Buses in Asia: Tips, Safety, Choosing a Seat, and What to Expect." Updated May 30, 2018. https://www.tripsavvy.com/buses-in-asia-1458391.

Rodgers, Greg. "Tips for Taking Night Buses in Asia: How to Survive an Overnight Bus in Asia." Updated May 26, 2019. https://www.tripsavvy.com/tips-for-taking-night-buses-4016895.

"Rolling With It: The Best Bus for Your Buck." The Washington Post. Accessed August 13, 2020. https://www.washingtonpost.com/wp-srv/artsandliving/travel/busreview/.

"Route Map." Alaska Railroad. Accessed August 29, 2020. https://www.alaskarailroad.com/ride-a-train/route-map.

Ryan. "Top 5 Public Transportation Systems in South America," *Go Backpacking* (blog). March 16, 2015, https://gobackpacking.com/public-transportation-south-america/.

Sam at EF. "3 Simple Tips for Riding the Metro in Europe." EF Educational Tours. Accessed September 24, 2020. https://blog.eftours.com/how-to/travel-tips/3-tips-for-riding-the-metro-in-europe.

Schrader, Robert. "Tokyo Metro: The Complete Guide." Updated June 26, 2019. https://www.tripsavvy.com/tokyo-metro-the-complete-guide-4685450.

Schwieterman, Joe. "Can Bolt Bus and Megabus Carve into Amtrak's Market Share?" *Market Urbanism Report* (blog). September 14, 2018. https://marketurbanismreport.com/blog/can-bolt-bus-and-megabus-carve-into-amtraks-market-share.

Seemann, Katie. "The 13 Best Websites for Finding Cheap Car Rentals [2020]." As of July 25, 2020. https://upgradedpoints.com/best-websites-for-cheap-car-rentals/.

Seemann, Katie. "The 14 Best Websites for Booking Flights at the Cheapest Prices [2020]." As of July 21, 2020. https://upgradedpoints.com/best-websites-for-booking-cheap-flights.

Sheehy, Kelsey. "The Cheapest Way to Rent a Car: 10 Tips." March 9, 2017. https://www.nerdwallet.com/article/finance/find-cheap-car-rental.

"Shuttle Service – Groome Transportation – Book Now." Groome Transportation. Accessed March 18, 2021. https://groometransportation.com/#gt-locations-2.

Soul Drifters. *24+ Adrenaline Junkie Bucket List Adventures* (blog). As of June 2019. https://souldrifters.com/adrenaline-pumping-adventures/.

"South America/Practical Information/Transport/Getting Around/Bus." Lonely Planet. Accessed November 14, 2020. https://www.lonelyplanet.com/south-america/narratives/practical-information/transport/getting-around/bus.

South East Asia Backpacker. "Book Local Transport in Southeast Asia." Timetables & Booking: Search Buses, Trains & Boats in Southeast Asia. Accessed November 6, 2020. https://southeastasiabackpacker.com/plan-your-trip/book-bus-train-ferry-tickets/.

"Southeast Asia/Practical Information/Transport/Getting Around." Lonely Planet. Accessed November 15, 2020. https://www.lonelyplanet.com/southeast-asia/narratives/practical-information/transport/getting-around.

Stanborough, Rebecca Joy. "6 Science-Supported Benefits of Thai Massage." Written July 14, 2020. https://www .healthline.com/health/thai-massage-benefits#bottom-line.

Steph. "11 Things You Need to Know about Bus Travel in Central America." Big World Small Pockets. Published December 17, 2016; last modified July 21, 2020. http:// web.archive.org/web/20200809022349/https://www.bigwo rldsmallpockets.com/bus-travel-central-america.

Steves, Rick. "Europe's Long-Distance Buses." Accessed September 24, 2020. https://www.ricksteves.com/travel -tips/transportation/boats-buses/long-distance-buses.

Steves, Rick. "Riding Europe's Subways." Accessed September 24, 2020. https://www.ricksteves.com/travel-tips /transportation/city-transit/riding-europes-subways.

"Shared Ride Shuttle." SuperShuttle. Accessed August 29, 2020. https://www.supershuttle.com/ride-choices/shared-ride -shuttle/.

"Taxes." Taxes in Belize of Mexico and Central America. Fodor's Travel. Accessed January 30, 2021. https:// www.fodors.com/world/mexico-and-central-america /belize/travel-tips/taxes-264933800#:~:text=When %20leaving%20Belize%20by%20land,in%20U.S .%20or%20Belize%20dollars.

Thomas, Edwin. "How to Rent Cars in Pakistan." January 15, 2019. https://traveltips.usatoday.com/rent-cars-pakistan -33597.html.

Tieso, Michael. "East Coast Buses: Megabus vs. Boltbus vs. Greyhound." *Why Wait to See the World?* (blog) March 19, 2013. https://whywaittoseetheworld.com/east-coast -buses-megabus-boltbus-greyhound/.

"Top 10 Benefits to Staying in a Bed and Breakfast."
Superpages. Accessed June 28, 2020. https://www
.superpages.com/em/top-10-benefits-bed-and-breakfast/.

Traub, Courtney. "Getting Around Paris: Guide to Public
Transportation." TripSavvy, Updated. April 27, 2020.
https://www.tripsavvy.com/how-to-use-paris-public
-transportation-1618925.

"Travel around Australia." Tourism Australia. Accessed
November 4, 2020. https://www.australia.com/en-us/facts
-and-planning/getting-around.html.

"The Ultimate Guide to Bus Travel in Africa." Where the Road
Forks: An Adventure Travel & Outdoors Blog. June 8,
2019. https://wheretheroadforks.com/the-ultimate-guide-to
-bus-travel-in-africa/.

"USA/Practical Information/Transport/Getting Around." Lonely
Planet. Accessed December 13, 2020. https://www
.lonelyplanet.com/usa/narratives/practical-information
/transport/getting-around.

"U.S. to Mexico Cross-Border Car Rental." Budget Car Rental.
Accessed September 4, 2020. https://www.budget.com/en
/help/usa-faqs/cross-into-mexico.

"U.S. to Canada Cross-Border Car Rental." Budget Car Rental.
Accessed September 4, 2020. https://www.budget.com/en
/help/usa-faqs/cross-into-canada.

"Use Uber in Cities around the World." Uber Cities – Rides
Around the World | Uber. Accessed October 7, 2020.
https://www.uber.com/global/en/cities/.

"Wellness Practices Around the World – 21 Self-Care Ideas."
Travel Bliss Now. November 1, 2020. https://www
.travelblissnow.com/wellness-practices/.

"What Are the Pros and Cons of Staying in A Bed and
Breakfast?" Select Registry. August 28, 2018. https://
selectregistry.com/blog/pros-and-cons-of-a-bed-and
-breakfast/.

"What Is Food Tourism?" World Food Travel Association.
Accessed July 11, 2020. https://worldfoodtravel.org/what
-is-food-tourism-definition-food-tourism/.

Welcome to Guiding Architects. Guiding Architects. Accessed
July 12, 2020. https://www.guiding-architects.net/wp
-content/uploads/2018/12/GA_Flyer_A5_Web.pdf.

"Where We Are." Grab. Accessed October 17, 2020. https://
www.grab.com/sg/locations/.

"Why Stay at a B&B?" Vrbo. Accessed June 28, 2020.
https://www.bedandbreakfast.com/info/travelers/travel
-inspiration-guides/why-choose-bed-and-breakfasts/.

Yip, Stephanie, and Dawn Daniels. "Uber vs. Taxi: Which One
Is the Better Option in 2021?" finder.com, Updated April
27, 2020. https://www.finder.com/uber-vs-taxi.

Zakhareuski, Andrei. "6 Things to Know About International
Driver's License (a.k.a. International Driving Permit)"
Driving Tests, Updated November 4, 2020. https://driving
-tests.org/beginner-drivers/international-drivers-license/.

Zimmermann, Kim Ann. "What Is Culture?" July 12, 2017.
https://www.livescience.com/21478-what-is-culture
-definition-of-culture.html.

Please Review this Book!

If you enjoyed *The Travel Champion: A 4-Step Guide to Traveling the World Solo, Safely, and on a Budget*, please consider providing a review on Amazon. It would be greatly appreciated. Reviews help authors more than you may realize. Thank you in advance!

Write a Customer Review on Amazon US

Write a Customer Review on Amazon UK

About the Author

Cicely F. Mitchell absolutely loves to travel! She is proclaimed The Travel Champion because she is a passionate proponent for all things related to travel and has extensive experience conquering the world as a solo, budget traveler. Currently, she has visited all fifty U.S. states, all seven continents, and over thirty countries. Nearly 90 percent of the trips she planned herself and over two-thirds of her international travel was achieved solo. Regardless of her income at the time of each trip, Ms. Mitchell stayed within her budget and had some truly amazing and memorable experiences. Throughout her three decades of travel, she has learned tremendous amounts of information, hacks, and tips that she is enthusiastic about sharing with aspiring and seasoned travelers alike.

Aside from traveling, Cicely is active in her church, community, and Delta Sigma Theta Sorority, Incorporated. By profession, she is an engineer, educator, and real estate investor. An advocate of education and lifelong learning, Cicely is a proud alumna of Tennessee State University, Purdue University, and Penn State University.

For more information, visit https://linktr.ee/thetravelchampion or contact info@thetravelchampion.com.

Engage with Cicely F. Mitchell on social media:

Follow on Amazon Author Central:
https://www.amazon.com/author/thetravelchampion

Follow on Instagram:
https://instagram.com/thetravelchampion

Like on Facebook:
https://facebook.com/thetravelchampion

Follow on TikTok:
https://tiktok.com/@thetravelchampion

Follow on Twitter:
https://twitter.com/thetravelchamp

Follow on Clubhouse:
https://joinclubhouse.com/thetravelchamp

Subscribe on YouTube:
https://www.youtube.com/channel/UCMb9hoN8J3de6qQmi0wtcvg